Alabama Buttermilk

Alabama BUTTERMILK

The Making of a Humble Hero

Alvin 'Alabama' Lovett

Walk By Faith Publishing
www.wbyf.site

Alabama Buttermilk - The Making of a Humble Hero

Author - Alvin 'Alabama' Lovett
Preliminary Work by - Rainelle Saunders
Compiled by - Joyce Eberhardt-Lovett
Adapted by - Dorcas Allen
Developmental Editor - Barbara Wolfe
Graphic Design - Frederick Allen

ISBN: 978-1-972760-04-8

Published in the United States by Walk By Faith Publishing, a division of Walk By Faith Worldwide. www.wbyf.site

This is my story—where I came from, what I've been through, and how I'm still standing. It's real, it's raw, and it's from the heart.

Visit our website at alabamabuttermilk.com

Table of Contents

ABOUT THE AUTHOR

Alvin Louis Lovett, affectionately known as Alvin Alabama Lovett, was born and raised in the vibrant city of Mobile, Alabama. As a respected philanthropist, he has made significant contributions through community service and his expertise in salesmanship. Alvin has dedicated his life to helping others uncover their purpose and achieve success. After spending over three decades in a city called Compton, California, he has returned to Mobile to enjoy his retirement years while continuing to spread the empowering message of his book, which centers on achieving victory in life.

With a wealth of experience as a historian, Alvin is celebrated for his exceptional storytelling abilities and profound memory, often regarded as a walking encyclopedia. His talents have earned him recognition from politicians, city officials, and celebrities. However, Alvin takes even greater pride in being acknowledged by everyday people, such as the person at the corner stop sign or the family under the bridge, who value his unique insights and captivating stories.

Alvin's journey has been marked by numerous ups and downs, reminding others that success is still attainable despite life's challenges. His experiences, captured in his book, are filled with angels and heroes—often unnoticed by many, yet brought into one's life by divine intervention when needed the most. He emphasizes the importance of humility and grace, encouraging others to keep expressions like "please," "I'm sorry," and "please forgive me" in their vocabulary. This embodies a testament to love and faith in God, trusting that His plan, although it may not align with personal visions, is ultimately the best.

In his leisure time, Alvin cherishes moments with his family and remains committed to supporting others. He diligently maintains contact with everyone in his phone log, reflecting his dedication to nurturing strong relationships. Alvin's mission is to inspire individuals to live courageously and authentically, sharing practical stories of personal growth and transformation from his life's journey.

Always Keep Dreaming

Alvin encourages everyone to hold on to their dreams. His words serve as a reminder to continue pursuing aspirations with determination and faith. His life and work exemplify the power of dreams and the importance of perseverance in achieving goals. In the spirit of his unwavering belief, Alvin's journey is a testament to the truth that dreams can indeed become reality when pursued with passion and resilience.

FOREWORD I

When I agreed to write a foreword for such an incredible human being, which, let's be honest, isn't something you typically get to do in the automotive industry, I had no idea how profound our first meeting would turn out to be. It was a cold, rainy spring morning on a car lot in Carson, California. I'll never forget it.

Truthfully, I feel a little embarrassed writing this. After all, he stuck it out through the ups and downs of car sales much longer than I ever did.

Part of me thinks someone from management at one of the dealerships he worked at could have written something more polished, more eloquent, and certainly with more detail than I could.

But if Alabama wants to use this book to inspire and motivate others - if he wants to share his powerful, unique journey that I experienced, starting with our hours-long conversation practically on Day One, in that space between the Chrysler Jeep Dodge and Lincoln-Mercury lot- then I believe readers will feel the weight of what one real, meaningful conversation can do. How it can shift a life.

I believe that's what he's done here. Although my career path ultimately led to me making a manufacturing-level brand impact, we've stayed connected over the years. We've also trained together in the dealerships for many years ever since. I made sure anything he and I were talking about were being communicated about directly to the executives at the multinational level. His words are powerful.

Alabama epitomizes "Movement That Inspires." He has a heart of gold, and a burning desire to help others. To anyone who cares about the relationship side of this, or any other industry, you already know: miscommunication is where the disconnect often lives.

Multiply that across thousands of missed opportunities- just in Southern California alone- and you'll understand how much is lost when car sales aren't anchored in real connection. Customers and dealerships alike suffer when there's no honest handshake, no genuine rapport. That's the cost of disconnection.

But Alabama was, and still is, a cut above that. His communication skills transcend ordinary levels. I imagine there are a lot of lizards all over Los Angeles County who were probably relieved to hear he retired.

But I doubt they'll be able to beat the consistent ethical sales success he created, year after year. It's the reason why he was #1 in Los Angeles, the nation and (I'll say it because he's so humble, but other people need to hear it) the world.

His entire career stood on one powerful principle. He was in the trenches turning wrenches, proving it over and over again, breaking every norm of traditional car sales and documenting it meticulously.

Here's that principle: Business isn't business. Business is people.

Alabama is, and always has been, a community builder. That alone gave him an edge, a deep understanding of the human condition.

He didn't just sell vehicles. He saw people reaching for help, and helping them through that sale was both an honor and a privilege to him.

Of all the sales industries, car sales might be the most fascinating. It draws in the gambler's mind. I've known plenty of car guys (and girls) who got addicted to the action and the dopamine rush, only to burn out and leave because their interactions were too transactional.

You can smell commission breath from a mile away. Alabama was never like that. He was just as precise and professional to others as he is humble, and humanitarian to many.

To the aspiring sales professional reading this: don't call it a "book." Call it a "course of study." It's a deep look into Alabama's life and the lens he used to lead with purpose, communicate effectively, and serve the community as a moral compass for human relationships.

He's walking you through the game of life on many levels. If more people study this book through the lens of service rather than transaction, I believe we'll witness a shift in how business is done. A new ecosystem will emerge, one where car dealers, local communities, and facilitators like Alabama work together to build stronger relationships and create more meaningful human interactions that have long, lasting impact.

And, that bright, fresh perspective? It's just as exciting as that new car smell. But even better? Having a friend in the car business, not just a friendly car salesman.

Instead of surface-level conversations and forgettable interactions, you'll start to see stories being shared at the delivery bay. You'll hear invites to barbecues, and feel what it means to be welcomed into someone's world and will refer to others, not just handed keys to a car.

Alabama, I consider you a great friend. It's truly an honor to write this foreword for such an extraordinary individual.

I never imagined that the same car lot where I once cut my teeth on the finance and insurance side would one day be the setting for one of the most important, prolific, long-term friendships of my life.

Thank you for your service. And thank you for all you've done, for the community, for the people, and for the future of this business.

Fred Smith, NewRoom Collective

FOREWORD II

'Alabama' is married to my cousin Joyce, and I met him when they started dating. My first encounter with 'Alabama' is probably similar to everyone's first encounter with 'Alabama'. One thing is how tall he is and how effervescent and friendly he is. He's the kind of person who wants to know everyone he meets. He wants to know who you are. What makes you happy? That struck me about him. Another thing that struck me is that, other than my close family, he's the only person in the family who, every time I see him, would be curious and excited and grateful for the work I do with HIV/AIDS. I think that today more people are comfortable talking about the subject, and there are still many who are uncomfortable.

Even back then, 'Alabama' was never hesitant in his curiosity. He was always asking questions and would always say, 'I follow your work. Congratulations, and thank you for the work that you do". That was at a time when many people were still shy about even raising the notion of HIV/AIDS. 'Alabama' would always ask me if there was a way that he could help. One evening there was a family dinner with him, Joyce, my partner, and me. We were talking about issues surrounding the black community. I said that there are so many people walking around who don't know their HIV status. We needed to find a way to help black people, particularly in South Los Angeles, because they are disproportionately impacted in Los Angeles County. If we could get them to be willing to get tested, it would be an incentive. They could get tested and have a raffle where they could win a new car. 'Alabama' said it was a great idea and that he could make that happen. He went back to the management at Car Pros Kia of Carson and then talked to the owner, Ken Phillips. He was able to convince him to donate a car as part of our raffle to encourage people to get tested for HIV/AIDS. We ran that program for three years. Beyond the testing over the years, we expanded it to have people increase their knowledge, and it became quite a remarkable awareness campaign, and the only campaign of its kind, targeting black people, in the country.

'Alabama' engages enthusiastically in everything he does. It wasn't enough for him to donate a car to help raise awareness for HIV/AIDS. He became an ambassador. Everywhere he went, he talked to people about paying attention to AIDS, and the importance of knowing their status. He took an HIV test in public, which was impactful. He joined the Black AIDS Institute in the King Day Parade and the Compton Christmas Parade. He met people who needed help or could help us in our work and he referred them to us. He's a connector who connects people and causes to each other.

I was diagnosed with HIV very early on in the epidemic. There is a unique connection with me being an advocate, an activist, a policy maker, and a person living with HIV. At the same time, I was a special assistant to Mayor Tom Bradley and ran all of the HIV/AIDS programs for the City of Los Angeles for many years. I was the first Co-Chair of the LA County HIV Health Counsel. I was a presidential appointment of President Clinton and President Obama on the topic. The fact is that I have served in the role of a person living with HIV. Being an advocate, being an activist, being a policy maker and being a clinical provider with the AIDS Institute, I have been able to see the epidemic from all of its perspectives." - *Phill Wilson*

PREFACE

Have you ever been called a hero? And, if so, did you hesitate to accept such a lofty title? Was it because you know the simple truth is that you are merely a humble soldier of the Lord? Did you feel a little undeserving of the praise because you know how bumpy the road has been? I have to be honest. People have sometimes referred to me as a hero and, trust me, that road has had many bends and turns and potholes along the way, and also many glorious heights. I certainly don't see myself as a hero. I must confess that God is my hero. His love is present in everything that I do, and the work that I do is a reflection of His Amazing Grace. If someone sees me as a person who lives to serve his fellow man -- a person who would not give up on himself or others -- a giver who shines a bit of hopeful light at the end of a dark tunnel -- then I'm happy to be that person. If I do some of those things each day, then I am truly made in God's image. There's nothing wrong with that. Nothing at all.

As amazing as my life has been, with all of its many blessings, it wasn't always a walk in the park. It was often interrupted by hard lessons and misguided choices. I don't know how you feel about it, but challenging moments like that are great times for reflection. Moments that create opportunities for us to grow and give us reasons to renew our faith. But, heroic? Not quite. I'm here to share my personal story. I'll give you the good, the bad, and the sometimes ugly. It's important to know that there is no shame in living a full life, especially when valuable lessons are learned and redemption is the reward. I am proud of where the winding road has taken me, the incredible journey that God lovingly prepared for me, and the opportunity to be of service to so many people. I have loved and praised the Lord throughout the course of this glorious journey. I imagine that someone can learn a few things from reading the story of my life. Always put God first, give to others whenever you are able, and never stop believing in your divine destiny. Thank you for picking up this book and walking down memory lane with this humble Alabama man.

Alvin Louis Lovett

CHAPTER 1

The Name That Carried a City

The Legacy and Community of the Lovett Family

In Mobile, Alabama, the Lovett name was everywhere. It is now, always was, and always will be an honor to be a Lovett.Growing up, I saw my family as unique—set apart in a special way. People around the city often thought we were well-off. In reality, we were a hardworking, middle-class family. But the name carried weight.

The Lovett name was a Mobile tradition. That's because my family ran the local funeral home—with our name right on the sign. Everyone knew Lovett's Funeral Home.The original founder was my great-grandfather, Rev. Britt Mose (B.M.) Lovett. He built it with his sons—Frank, Mose, and William Lovett—and his daughter, Mary Lovett Williams. William Wiggins, his in-law, and Jiles Lovett, his adopted nephew, also helped shape the business.

Rev. B.M. Lovett was more than a businessman. He was a pastor, a spiritual leader to many Black Baptist churches across Mobile. He led Truevine Missionary Baptist Church for more than fifty years. To our family, and to many others, he was a guiding force.Maybe that's why people thought we were a big deal. It was all in the name.But here's the truth: we had no real wealth. The money stayed in the business.Still, none of that mattered. We were Lovetts. And being a Lovett meant something. It still does.

Rev. B.M. Lovett, the elder head of our family, lived at the last house on Plum Street—renamed Lovett Way in April 2019. He was a tall, good-looking man with a dark complexion and proud stature. A commanding presence, he led many church congregations with a firm, “do as I say” attitude. His voice carried authority, and his sermons seemed to hold people in a spiritual spell. I never saw him do much outside of talking about God and telling people what to do. In my eyes, he was the first Black man I ever saw exercising what felt like “white man powers”—strong influence, complete control, and unwavering respect.

His impact wasn’t limited to the pulpit or the public. It extended into our family life in more ways than one. His influence shaped our values, our name—and even our hairlines. He passed down the infamous Lovett receding hairline to the men in our family. Thanks a lot, sir. But truthfully, my great-grandfather was a great man. When I think of him, I remember that dominating personality and the legacy he left behind in all of us.

Truevine Missionary Baptist Church sat at the corner of Peach Street and Pecan Street, in a neighborhood known as The Bottom, just off Davis Avenue. Rev. B.M. Lovett led the church, but it was his wife, Mama Jettie Lovett, who quietly supported the ministry’s reach. Together, they served the community in practical ways. Rev. Lovett’s ministry provided fresh vegetables to local families, and Mama Jettie faithfully tended the lush garden behind their home. Neighbors also came to her for chickens and eggs—simple needs she met with steady care.

Mama Jettie was a sweet, soft-spoken woman of light complexion who lived in her husband’s shadow and did what was asked of her. She didn’t seek recognition but offered love through acts of quiet service. Her giving spirit touched many, and her presence was a blessing to neighbors from all over the area. She lived to be 105 years old. I was in my 30s when we lost her, but the memory of her gentle strength still stays with me.

Before settling in Mobile, Rev. B.M. Lovett served as pastor to more than ten churches across rural Alabama. His early ministry was shaped by constant travel and dedication to communities with limited resources.

After arriving in Mobile, he split his time between two congregations—preaching two Sundays a month at Truevine Missionary Baptist Church and the other two at Mt. Pleasant Baptist Church, located in an area known as Down the Bay. During the 1930s through the 1950s, few churches could afford to pay a full-time pastor, so many, like Rev. Lovett, relied on serving multiple congregations to make ends meet. In addition to regular preaching, he officiated weddings, led funeral services, and prayed for the sick—spiritual labor that helped sustain his income.

It was through this work, particularly his role in conducting funerals, that Rev. Lovett saw a greater need and opportunity. In 1941, just after the Great Depression, Lovett's Funeral Home opened its doors.

My grandfather, Mose Lovett, was the middle son. He worked as a longshoreman and a skilled carpenter. Standing just 5'8", he carried himself with quiet strength. Known for his honesty and integrity, he served as Treasurer and deacon at Truevine Missionary Baptist Church. He was also a talented baseball player, and one of my favorite memories is playing catch with him. Like many Lovetts, he was diabetic—something I suspect had to do with our family's diet. I remember him waking up around 4 a.m. to eat and take his insulin, a routine that showed his quiet discipline and resilience.

My grandmother, Afrey Rogers Lovett, was married to Mose. She was the daughter of Edith Cruz, a respected member of the Order of the Eastern Star—a title that carried great admiration in our community. Grandmother Afrey was wise with money; I used to call her my banker because she always managed finances so well. She was soft-spoken, graceful, and always beautifully dressed, a true representative of our family's dignity. Her sister, Ruth, had seventeen children. Lord have mercy!

My grandfather's youngest son, William "Uncle Willie" Lovett, was one of the most visionary businessmen of his time. He successfully expanded the family enterprise by managing Lovett's Funeral Home with professionalism and care. Recognizing a deep need in the community, he established Lovett's Burial Insurance Company to help families cover the cost of funeral services. During a time when many struggled financially, the burial insurance plan provided a critical safety net, ensuring loved ones could be laid to rest with dignity. His leadership helped countless families navigate loss without the added burden of financial strain.

Beyond his business success, Uncle Willie was also deeply involved in the civil rights movement. He was known to post bail for protestors, helping them get out of jail when few others would step in. His contributions extended to hosting and supporting leaders like Dr. Martin Luther King Jr., who spent time in Mobile during the fight for justice. Uncle Willie used his resources, connections, and influence not only to serve the community in business but to stand on the right side of history.

Black-owned insurance companies were instrumental during the civil rights movement. Lovett Insurance Company was one of them. Through Lovett Insurance Company, Uncle Willie became the one who posted bail for many of the heroes who were jailed for their civil rights activities.

I was raised knowing I belonged to a family that did important work in the community. Grandfather Mose built the very first casket used at Lovett's Funeral Home. I admired him not just for his skill, but because he was a carpenter—like Jesus—which, in our Baptist family, held special significance. These were the heroes of my life. We were proud to be part of a thriving, purpose-driven family business that served with integrity and faith.

Colorism shaped burial practices in our community.

At a time when even death was not free from discrimination, Lovett's Funeral Home stood apart. Some funeral homes predominantly served lighter-skinned African Americans, denying dignity to those with darker complexions. But Lovett's provided respectful, dignified services to everyone—regardless of skin tone. This commitment allowed our family to serve grieving families from all parts of the community and uphold a standard of care rooted in equality and compassion.

Black Insurance Week in Mobile honored the Black-owned insurance companies that supported funeral homes like Lovett's. These companies helped families afford dignified burials and made it possible for funeral homes to serve the community with compassion and consistency.

During that time, a prominent African-American businessman named A. G. Gaston was involved in a funeral home business in Birmingham, Alabama, north of Mobile. Formed in a partnership with his father-in-law, A. L. Smith, the Smith & Gaston Funeral Home was started in 1938. Some said that

Arthur George Gaston was the richest black man in America. He owned several businesses and his companies employed a lot of black people in Alabama. One of his companies was the Booker T. Washington Insurance Company which he started in 1932. A. G. Gaston's influence was extensive, with business interests that included a bank, motel, construction company and a business school. He was also known for providing financial support to the building funds for several churches in Mobile. He also used his financial influence in the fight for civil rights in the 1960s. He died in 1996 at the age of 103. A. G. Gaston was a heroic figure for many, including me and my family.

The men in my family were also heroic men. I looked up to them because they were instrumental in providing good spirit in the church through prayer and services. They also went out among the community, visiting people, and helping the sick. I got a chance to meet and make associations with all kinds of people outside of my family by being a Lovett. I was proud to be called Lovett. I still am, and I thank God for Rev. B. M. Lovett and Mama Jettie Lovett for starting it all and being the incredible foundation of our family.

The Lovetts were more than just spiritual leaders—they were caretakers of the community. Rev. B.M. Lovett's yard featured a rare resource for the neighborhood: an outdoor toilet. At a time when many nearby homes lacked proper bathroom facilities, this simple structure offered more than just relief—it offered dignity.

Located at the end of Plum Street, the toilet became a hub of community interaction. Neighbors came by throughout the day, and Rev. Lovett used these moments to connect with them. As people waited their turn, he made conversation, shared encouragement, and often introduced them to Christ. What began as an act of hospitality became an extension of his ministry.

This daily outreach helped Truevine Missionary Baptist Church grow into one of the largest and most respected churches in Mobile. Rev. Lovett's vision wasn't just about powerful preaching—it was about meeting people where they were, with compassion, care, and practical support. That was part of his greatness—and his genius.

The neighborhood was filled with people from all walks of life – both famous and infamous. Behind Rev. Lovett's house lived a lady named Estella Payton. We knew her as 'Estelle'. She was the first

African-American who we saw regularly on television. To us, she was a person of significant status. For decades, she assisted with the cooking segments on the *Woman's World* TV show, which was a local show that aired on TV station WKRG Channel 5. WKRG was located near Davis Ave and was one of only two channels at that time. The other was WALA Channel 10. Estelle shared the *Woman's World* spotlight with a white woman named Connie Bea Hope. The long-running cooking show had its debut around 1955. Estelle began in '55 as Connie's assistant but never actually appeared on camera until the late '60s. Before that, only Estelle's hands would periodically be visible in a shot, as she set up or moved cooking utensils and handed over ingredients. It took years before Estelle was finally seen on-screen. She even received third billing in the shows' opening titles and was given a microphone! That microphone made it possible for her to answer Connie Bea while she was cooking, and to make the occasional comment.

Estelle was a beloved figure in both our church and our city. She had once been a co-star on a local TV show, which made her something of a celebrity in Mobile. For our family—and many others—seeing someone from our community on television was inspiring. It showed us what was possible. Estelle also had a special connection to greatness: she was the great-aunt of baseball legend Hank Aaron, another proud product of Mobile.

At Truevine Missionary Baptist Church, Estelle was more than a familiar face—she was a pillar. She served as a Matron and was active in the Baptist Sunlight District, offering her time and leadership generously. Some people even attended Truevine just to be near her, drawn by her warmth and quiet influence. Estelle was deeply loved, highly respected, and lived a long, meaningful life—reaching the golden age of 95.

CHAPTER 2

D-O, Not D-E: The Woman Called Dolores

The Woman Called Dolores

My parents, Britt Mose Lovett, Sr. and Dolores Williams Lovett, had three boys, which meant that they had their hands full. The first son was named Britt Mose Lovett, Jr., after my father. The middle son was named William LaGrand Lovett, and I was the baby, Alvin Louis Lovett. I was born on July 20, 1952. Our family was small, compared to my mother's.

My maternal grandparents were Rev. Ballard Williams and Alvenia Tate Williams. They had twelve children,six boys and six girls. My mother, Dolores, was number eight. When my mother was still young, Ballard left Alvenia with all of the children. He was not around during much of her life growing up, which was in an extremely poor area of Mobile. The children had to contribute to the family finances. In conversations with my mother, she would say that she might have been born in the ghetto, but she didn't want to live the life of someone in the ghetto. Everyone who met Dolores Williams Lovett saw a beautiful woman with pretty legs. She was petite, but she was also strong and with a beautiful shape. She could have been a model on the cover of a magazine. My mother was particular about people spelling her name correctly. She always insisted: "It's D-O-l-o-r-e-s, not D-E." A small but important correction, passed down from her mother, Alvenia.

My grandmother, Alvenia, had been the caretaker and housekeeper for my Uncle Willie and Aunt Lillian Lovett, who owned Lovett's Funeral Home. That's how my parents met.

They were teenagers when they fell in love and got married. My mother was close to her mother and learned the art of cooking. She furthered her culinary skills when she attended Josephine Allen Institute, a well-known private school in Mobile during the 1930s and 1940s, which was headed by a free black woman, Josephine Blackledge-Allen.

Some of my mother's sisters had as many as fifteen or sixteen children. Three of them lived in Birmingham and were very involved in the church. Like many others, I remember the infamous bombing of the 16th Street Baptist Church in Birmingham on September 15, 1963, where four young Black girls were killed.

That tragedy shook our entire family. It was a chilling reminder that even sacred places weren't safe for Black families. For me, it marked a turning point. I began to understand, in a deeply personal way, that standing up for civil rights could cost you your life—even as a child, even in church. The fear was real, but so was the need for change.

My mother always turned to her siblings for advice. Beyond Birmingham, they were spread across Detroit, New York, and here in Mobile—each representing another branch of our extended family. One of the most influential was Louis Clay Williams, the Vice Principal of Dunbar Junior High School in Mobile. He was the most accomplished of my mother's siblings, and one of my personal heroes. I can still hear his raspy yet powerful voice during school assemblies, declaring, "What you are going to be, you are now becoming!" He repeated that phrase every time he spoke. Decades later, I still carry those words with me.

My mother was a cook for South Central Bell Telephone Company for over 30 years. Throughout her career, she faced significant racial discrimination. In her later years at the company, she became a coin collector—a position she held due to her seniority.

When she was mistreated, I often wrote formal complaint letters on her behalf to advocate for fair treatment. Ultimately, South Central Bell laid her off under circumstances that strongly suggested discrimination, though it was never formally acknowledged.

Afterward, she continued doing what she loved—cooking. She took a position preparing meals for the priests at Spring Hill College, and later became the personal cook for Rev. Howard Johnson, pastor of Truevine Missionary Baptist Church.

Rev. Howard Johnson and his family went on to experience and share with the world some things in their lives which would become a part of our shared history itself. You see, Rev. Howard's only son, Howard Johnson II, deployed to Kuwait in February 2003 with other members of the Army's 507th Maintenance Company at Fort Bliss, in El Paso Texas. The deployment was to counter the efforts of al Qaeda, a faction of Iraqi fighters who were credited with the devastating 9/11 terrorist attacks upon our country. In March 2003 PFC Howard Johnson II was killed in an ambush by enemy forces, at his age 21. He was one of the first American casualties in Operation Iraqi Freedom, as well as the very first Alabama casualty. PFC Johnson II was posthumously awarded both the Bronze Star and the Purple Heart for his heroism. Other honors for the very patriotic young man would follow. The City of Mobile renamed a park in Mobile the Howard Johnson II Park. His mother, Gloria, who had looked forward to her son's return and working alongside her in her private school renamed the school PFC Howard Johnson II Academy and Children's Center. His family and many others continue to remember and celebrate the very loving and kind spirit who answered the call of duty in the service to America. Another of my heroes.

I was no more than five or six years old when we moved to 305 Adams Street between Jackson Street and Claiborne Street in Mobile. Our neighborhood was downtown near what was known as the French Quarter. Adams Street was one of the streets noted to be a boundary of the French Quarter and was, later, identified as the DeTonti Square Historic District. The historic district was named after Henri De Tonti who was a military officer and explorer who claimed lands for Louis XIV of France. Of course, I didn't know that at the time, but I understood that ours was a home of which my mother was very proud. She took a lot of pride in painting her house and planting flowers. We were known for the beautiful flowers in our home and yards. Mother was so pleased to see people come by to view her displays. She worked very hard to make sure that her house was going to be the most beautiful house in Mobile. That was her main goal.

Some years later, after a very significant relocation move to the Toulminville community, Dolores Lovett continued to have the most decorated yard in the entire area. At that time, she lived across from Good Shepherd Episcopal Church. She was able to build a beautiful home there. However, it seemed to me that her goals had grown as large as her beautiful plants. My mother wanted to be known for her beauty on the inside as well as her beauty on the outside. Along with that, she desired to go to glory when she died.

I was able to see many different sides to my mother. One side of her was soft and nurturing. The other side was a strict disciplinarian. She was like a prison warden. Of course, I had no idea what it was like to be in prison, but I often felt like my dreams were locked up. I was locked up inside my dreams. I had to find a way to express myself while still toeing the line for my mother. For reasons that I will explain later, she was overly protective of me, and I didn't like it.

My father was just as strict as my mother. He and I had a love/hate relationship because of the way he handled me and my brothers. Britt Sr. was a tall, muscular man who was left-handed and had played football in his past. He was known for being a good player. Britt, Sr. was, also, considered the black sheep of the family who didn't follow the traditional ways of the Lovetts. He was a gambler who liked to hang in the streets and have a good time. But he showed his darker side when it came to his three sons. He hit us too hard and was too forceful. He even taught us to lie. Like the time when a bill collector came to get his money, my father told me to say that he wasn't home. And that's exactly what I did. With my chest proudly poking out, I announced "My Daddy said to tell you that he isn't home." For that, my father beat the crap out of me. I was confused because we were supposed to be 'good boys', so right and so perfect. I spoke properly and told the truth. Thought he would be proud of me.

Since when was that wrong? I didn't understand him, so I just tried to stay away from him as much as possible.

As the oldest, Britt, Jr. was like another parent to LaGrand and me. Our parents trained him to discipline us when they weren't around. That means he also punished us like our parents did, except he was worse. He was a little shy in some ways, but he took advantage of us and turned into an evil twin when he was in charge. If there were cookies for all of us, he would beat us and eat all the cookies. It wasn't fair. On the other hand, he was very protective of us. I can honestly say that he would die for us. There was a lot of drama in my household back then. That will surprise people who knew me when I was a child. My family was thought to be the dream family. And we were perceived that way in public. But behind closed doors, we were very dysfunctional. My father beat my mother, too. We all suffered from physical and mental abuse. There were many times that Mama had to cover her bruises with powder and lipstick, but that didn't stop my mother from keeping her house immaculate. In her mind, she was a queen. Her way of cleaning was very detailed, and she punished us even if we didn't put the dishes away to her liking. My father was more relaxed about cleaning. My brothers and I had to maintain balance in a no-win situation. Our behavior was determined by which one of my parents gave the orders. My mother worked us like slaves. We had no choice. Having no girls in the household meant that we had to do all of the chores. Whatever my mother had to do, we had to do, including proper etiquette. Teaching her three boys was not easy. We even learned how to set a formal table. Despite the harshness of her methods, my mother's acts of tough love helped to prepare me for the world. I have to be honest, though. It just didn't seem fair. However, not having any sisters created a sense of mystery for me. It meant not knowing a lot about girls, and not being familiar with a female point of view other than that of my mother. I became curious about my life and many important things. I know that both of my parents meant well, and I'm sure that my mother's main goal was to prepare all of us to be our best, even though I was left with a few negative memories in my mind. I guess it was the same goal for my father too.

CHAPTER 3

When My Legs Failed, Their Arms Lifted Me

Unexpected Lessons of Pain, Vulnerability, and Recovery

My family and I faced adversity when I was five. I developed a health problem, which made it impossible for me to see my life in the same way. They said it was "polio-like" but they didn't know. Looking back, they might have misdiagnosed me. It could have been a bone disease or vitamin D deficiency like rickets. Who knows what it was? One day, I couldn't walk like the other boys. My parents should have taken me to a doctor, but that's not something they did. For them, it would have been extreme, and they never wanted to appear hysterical or anything other than the 'perfect family'. They didn't run to get help every time there was illness or injury like the white folks did with their kids. Isn't that something? Were we really supposed to believe the myth and misconception that black people don't feel as much pain as white people? That we have a higher tolerance for suffering? That's not true! We do suffer. We suffer from many things, including our lack of knowledge and our lack of faith.

I became the burden child that everyone carried around because I couldn't walk on my own. That sounds like a bad thing, and I'm not saying that it wasn't a challenge. It was. But, because of my physical limitations, I was given other advantages. I was able to see everything at different levels. I experienced the world around me through the eyes of the aunts, uncles, and cousins who were willing to carry me in their arms, and on their backs and shoulders. What a blessing they all were to me. My parents eventually had to do something about the fact that my legs weren't working. The result was not pleasant. I ended up having to wear braces like Forrest Gump. As a child, it's important to develop self esteem through your physicality. My condition made me feel insecure. I couldn't run as fast or jump as high as the other boys. Wearing leg braces shaped my self-concept, which is so important. When you are impaired, it presents a challenge, and that was one of my earliest challenges. I was often not picked to play sports, and if so, I was the last one on the roster. I know that many of us can relate to that feeling of not being wanted. The shame of feeling like we are invisible, even in a crowd of people. Looking back, I am grateful to my family for seeing that I was special. They helped me find my voice. Because of that, I was able to reach thousands of people on television years later. That was a milestone to reach as a kid who grew up in a poor neighborhood.

Even before the braces, there was another crisis I had as a small child. I was told that when I was 2 or 3 years old I guess I found the packaging on the bottle of mom's bleach attractive and it was easy for me to just turn it up and drink it. My parents had to rush me to the hospital. I didn't know then but bleach poisoning can cause diarrhea, a sore throat, and slurred speech. A person could even slip into a coma and not be able to breathe. Thank God there was no permanent damage. As I got older, I thought I had two birthmarks on my stomach, but it was where tubes were inserted there at the hospital. I have to say that when it came to health scares, I kept my parents busy. I continued to find mischief that led to other ailments and I experienced a lot of injuries as a child.

One day, they replaced the leg braces with therapeutic boots, which I wore until I was eight. During my years of recovery and healing, it took the whole village to help care for me. My ailment impacted the entire family and my neighborhood. We were handed lemons, and we made lemonade. We also made lemon cookies and some lemon meringue pie! That's what the Lovetts did well. My family was very colorful. They took me all over the city. I saw places people didn't go. I saw things that most people didn't see. I met lots of unique people and was influenced by them. My affliction turned out to be a blessing in disguise.

Despite the challenges that I faced, there was a time when I realized how charming I could be. For that reason, I never wanted to miss a chance to go with my Mama to the beauty parlor on Beauregard Street. I often went there to be around the women and to entertain them while they were getting their hair pressed with those old, hot straightening combs. The smell of that hot grease sizzling and smoking their hair into an unnatural state is memorable. But that's what it took to make them all feel beautiful. Lucky for me, that process took quite a bit of time, which allowed me to do my thing. I don't mean to sound boastful at all, but let me tell you - I had some skills that people appreciated. I wasn't strong, but someone could take me on their hip and carry me to do my entertaining in front of as many as ten women. It's where I learned to talk in front of people. My brothers were athletic and could do a lot of other things, but they couldn't do what I could do. Everyone has their gifts, right? Some of my favorite people would be there. Cousin Tee, Cousin Jettie, and Miss Ruth loved watching me dance and sing. In return, they gave me pennies and nickels. That was the beginning of my hustle. Sometimes I preached up a storm by doing a Rev. B. M. Lovett sermon for their pleasure. They loved to hear me preach! It gave me confidence that I didn't have before. I performed to the best of my ability and took my offerings to buy myself some ice cream.

I mentioned that I took many trips to doctors and emergency rooms. It seems like I always gave my parents a reason to be on high alert. When it came to me and all the mischief that I managed to get into, I know that they were always expecting me to get into trouble. I think that my early years of being confined in those leg braces created a need for me to go a little wild once I was free. One time, I hit the front of my leg on a fan. That nasty little incident put a dent in the bone of my right tibia. Then I developed an infection in the shinbone, which created a high fever. While in a daze, I saw visions that I still remember to this day. Visions that inspired me and motivated me to be what I wanted to be. Eventually, I got stronger and began to run. Then I got faster, passing people who ran with me. I may have had a lot of setbacks in my life, but I realized that, no matter what, I have to keep getting up. Just because you lay down, doesn't mean you have to stay down.

Miss Gloria Jones, who we called 'Miss Beauty', had a daughter named Daviette Phillips (later, Daviette Ramos). She was my favorite friend at that time and one of the greatest clarinet players I ever heard. She was the one who allowed me to play a hero, like the ones I saw on television. One of my great opportunities to see a hero on TV was by watching Tarzan. Like him, I would swing and jump from tree to tree. When I played Tarzan, Daviette was my Jane. I was invincible, just like my hero. One day I jumped from a sycamore tree near Adams Street and Claiborne Street. When I jumped, a weak limb broke under my weight. On my way to the ground, a protruding nail ripped my right arm open. Daviette was right there to comfort me. She helped me through some of my worst injuries. After my fall, I was bleeding. I didn't know it at the time because I was wearing a red, long-sleeved shirt. Brushing off the incident, I left Daviette to run and find my friends who were playing football down the block. Someone chose me to be on their street team. As the game proceeded, we noticed that everyone's shirts were getting bloody. It didn't take long to discover that the blood was coming from my shirt and the wound on my arm. I'm still not sure why I didn't feel any pain, but I realized that even heroes had to go to the hospital to get stitches, especially when they are bleeding all over their friends. We were boys in a poor area, and we all found ways to express manhood. It was not easy to prove ourselves, show off our prowess, or be the Kings of the Jungle. Just like with the leg braces, I realized that injuring my right arm affected my thoughts about myself, as well as my physicality. It was important for young, black boys to be strong and smart. There weren't a lot of opportunities for us. We had to make it out any way we could, but we had to make it. That was the most important thing.

When I think about my friend Daviette I have to call her a Hero or Shero, if I'm to be politically correct. I fully recognize that she was a really good friend to me. I can't say the same about me. You see, Daviette was always in some trouble with her mother. When it was time for her to get a whipping, she tried to run away. I got so confident in my running that I liked to chase Daviette. She was fast and gave me a good workout. When I would eventually catch her, I would bring her back to her mother to get whipped. As a reward, Miss Beauty would pay me. I was all about getting my money so that I could get my treats! I would buy some of my favorite ice cream, some coffee rolls, or "two for a penny" cookies from Miss Teresa's convenience store, which was in my neighborhood at the corner of Lipscomb Street and Claiborne Street. Miss Teresa was a white woman who ran the store with her sister. I was a bounty hunter and buying those treats was a huge reward. I was selfish and felt so proud that I could run. But turning Daviette over to her mother for a whipping, just so that I could get paid, is still one of my greatest regrets.

As a teenager, Daviette had an opportunity to become one of the world's greatest clarinet players. She admits that she got sidetracked and ended up hooked on drugs, to the point of IV drug use. Fortunately, that road to destruction didn't last for long. Daviette was raised in a strong, spiritual family. They worshiped at the State Street AME Zion Church. She credits her faith with being put back on the right track and allowing her to live a positive life, eventually becoming a great mother. Daviette's heroic recovery also allowed her to help others caught up in the web of addiction by Simply sharing her own journey and, as she says, "Talking to folks". Sheroism in action my friends! Later in life, I had to ask Daviette for forgiveness. I confessed to her that I never realized how my attitude and bounty hunter actions were causing her such pain. I am humbled and appreciate that, like the friend she will forever be, she forgave me.

There were other times that I know I caused pain for others. It doesn't feel good to come clean about all of the harm you have done to so many. I can only take some solace in the fact that I tried to make amends. Did I see or hear apologies in my Family? Honestly, I don't know. I know that some people never apologize. I'm happy that I've taken opportunities to do that in my life. It's part of healing- mine and theirs- and it doesn't cost a thing.

In the part of Mobile that I'm from, life was different for us than for those living in other parts of Alabama. For instance, Birmingham was about the steel mills and the coal industry in the northern part of the state. Mobile, an international city, is on the water, and there were a lot of fisheries in the area. We ate a lot of fish. Learning how to avoid swallowing bones was important. With my big appetite, I always tried to eat fast so no one would take the food from me. It was competitive. The faster you eat, the more you get a chance to eat. One day I was tearing up some good fish and rushed to eat it, as usual. This time I messed up and swallowed a sharp fish bone. I got rushed to Mobile General Hospital, which was a segregated (white) hospital at the time. I waited so long, and was so uncomfortable, that I tried to get the bone out myself. I tried reaching down my throat and all sorts of things. I couldn't get that fish bone out of my throat! They say that you can swallow bread and drink water to push the bone down or loosen it. That was a 'home remedy' medical treatment back in the fifties. But I couldn't even swallow, which was a traumatic psychological experience. I thought my life was ending right then and there. The pain was excruciating because the bone had scratched the inner lining of my throat and pierced a significant hole in my esophagus. I did not feel whole and healthy. I had to compensate for my shortcomings. There were things that I could not do as I was healing. Being in this state of physical weakness gave me a psychological awareness that I wasn't invincible. I wasn't like Popeye the Sailor Man, my favorite cartoon hero character. He ate spinach and became strong. I wanted to be like him because of his ability to attract girls like Olive Oyl. He had challenges with Bluto and still came out a winner. I wanted to be that way, too. I had no idea that a little fish bone could impair the confidence I had in my physical abilities for my future.

I didn't know it then, but there would come a time when children would spend long hours on their cell phones and other devices playing games. Just as I believed in the cartoons played on television in the 50's, like me, those children would not know that much of what they saw on their devices were not real. Their parents and other adults in their lives would need to be carefully observant of what their children are experiencing, even while they are in our presence. Their fears, egos, and self-images are being shaped while they are engaged with toys, games, images on their devices - and food!

CHAPTER 4

Neighborhood Royalty

The Lovett Brothers

My mother always dreamed that all her children would learn how to swim. That dream came from her own childhood experience. As a young girl, she once snuck off to the local pool while my grandmother, Alvenia, was at work. She had hoped to return home before being discovered—but Grandma got there first. The scolding she received was so intense, it left a lasting mark. She never went swimming again. From that day forward, she made a vow: her children would grow up knowing how to swim.

True to her word, she took the three of us to the Davis Avenue Community House, the first public facility built for Black residents during segregation. After long days working at South Central Bell, she'd gather us in the evenings and head straight to the pool. The center also had tennis courts and a small park, but we were focused on one thing—the Davis Avenue Swimming Pool. That's where we learned, thanks to Donald "The Barracuda" Brown, who ruled that pool with energy and care. He was a remarkable teacher.

The Davis Avenue facility was expanded in 1936 and renamed the Davis Avenue Recreation Center. It still stands today beside the old Central High School—my alma mater—which has since been transformed into a training center for future nurses. Nearby is the Franklin Primary Health Center, founded in 1975 by concerned citizens who recognized the lack of healthcare in the area, especially for poor families of color. I'm proud to say I played a small role in the efforts that led to the repurposing of the high school and the establishment of that much-needed health center.

A lot has changed in the neighborhood, but the Davis Avenue pool is where my brothers and I first learned to swim. Later, as a Boy Scout, I completed a five-mile swim—something I was proud of. My brothers were strong swimmers, too. We each competed in different age groups and held our own at meets across the Mobile area.

We mastered a range of strokes—freestyle, backstroke, breaststroke, American crawl, and sidestroke—and earned several medals along the way. As a trio, we were a force in both scouting and local swim competitions. Swimming wasn't just a sport for us—it was a source of confidence, discipline, and pride.

Living in a family of competitive boys, with a mother who pushed us to do more, we stood out in the neighborhood. My brother LaGrand was the best looking of the three of us—charming, easygoing, and well-liked by everyone. Each of us had our own appeal, but our mother made sure we were different from other boys in the community. With no sisters in the house, we took on all the chores, including the ones usually assigned to girls. We dusted furniture, washed and dried dishes, waxed floors on our knees, and even learned to sew holes in our clothes. We painted, ironed, folded laundry, and kept the house in order. While other boys were out playing football with their friends, we were scrubbing and straightening. It gave us a different kind of discipline—and made us stand out among the kids on our block.

Still, I couldn't do the basic chores my brothers handled so easily. I couldn't even take out the trash. Raking leaves, earning allowance money, or trying to impress our parents through physical effort—those things were out of reach for me. My body didn't move the way theirs did. I couldn't run fast. I couldn't compete. Deep down, I felt like God had done me wrong by not giving me the same physical abilities. That pain was hard to admit, and even harder to carry, especially when I couldn't complain about the same things they did.

Being the youngest of three competitive boys came with its challenges. My brothers, Britt Jr. and LaGrand, were independent in ways I wasn't. Their world moved faster—literally. I couldn't keep up with their pace, and I was often left behind when we played or explored together. I was never as old, as fast, or as strong. So, I had to find my own identity. That search for self-discovery became central to who I was.

There were many things my brothers did well. Britt, in particular, excelled in writing and naturally stepped into leadership roles. Watching him succeed academically inspired me to push myself intellectually. He was the "experimental child"—the one our parents tested all their ideas and expectations on. LaGrand and I paid close attention. We learned what to emulate and what to avoid. We saw his successes, but we also saw the trouble he got into—and the consequences that followed.

Discipline in our household was serious. There was no leniency, no second chances, and certainly no outside support to soften the blow. Back then, there was no Oprah Winfrey on television offering empathy, and no social services to call. There were no laws protecting children from corporal punishment. If you stepped out of line, you got whipped—plain and simple. And no one wanted to face the wrath of our mother.

The beatings left welts on our bodies. That was abuse—our accepted form of punishment. We came to school with bruises, and I often assumed that other children's parents were going through their own struggles, taking it out on their kids. Whipping defined our way of life.

Looking back, I now understand the deeper impact that kind of discipline had on us. At the time, we didn't have the language or awareness to question it. Today, we know there are healthier ways to guide and correct children. But the truth is, we were all shaped—often harmed—by those experiences, passed down through generations. Our ancestors endured beatings and trauma in this country for hundreds of years. In many ways, their pain still echoes through us. Their souls still cry out.

In our community, official police presence was scarce; most neighborhoods policed themselves. I witnessed painful things in my own home, including moments when my father struck my mother. She often fought back, and he would leave the house. But the cycle was deeply unsettling.

Sadly, domestic violence was common in many households around us. Just as children were routinely whipped, women often suffered in silence. And when violence occurred, there were rarely consequences. No one went to jail. If one Black person harmed another—especially behind closed doors—it was overlooked. But the rules changed entirely if a white person was involved. Then, the punishment was swift and severe: prison, life sentences, even execution. That contrast was clear, and deeply unjust.

There is a long-standing disparity in sentencing when it comes to violence in Black communities. I grew up watching people fall into that trap. On Friday nights, many folks would get off work and head straight to the bars. With few opportunities and plenty of frustration, they often took their anger out on each other. Poverty, systemic racism, and the absence of consequences for harming other Black people created an environment where senseless violence felt almost expected. In the eyes of a racist legal system, these murders often went unpunished—as if Black lives mattered less.

That kind of violence is deeply connected to untreated trauma and mental illness, especially in underserved communities. People were hurting, and without access to care or support, their pain turned inward—and too often, outward. Poverty wasn't just about money; it was about despair, isolation, and a lack of vision for the future. The psychological toll continues today, affecting families in ways that are still not fully acknowledged.

But in the midst of that struggle, there was also extraordinary beauty. The greatest love I've ever seen has come from Black people loving each other—through struggle, joy, grief, and celebration. Our communities are full of creativity, resilience, and connection that can't be found anywhere else. Even with hardship, we've always known how to come together. Whether through laughter, a shared meal, or a helping hand, there's a sacred thread that links us to one another.

Parenting has evolved over the years, but the core remains the same: caring deeply for our children and guiding them with love. It used to be that anyone in the neighborhood could discipline a child—now, you offer a heads-up to the parents instead. We drive our kids to activities, cook meals with love, throw parties, and teach them the values that shape who they become. And while each child must forge their own path, they need a foundation—something spiritual, steadying, and strong. I can offer them the faith that guided me. My relationship with God has been my anchor. But in the end, every child must discover their own source of strength, because we are each just small pieces in something much greater than ourselves.

CHAPTER 5

Born Different, Raised Aware

Learning Social Injustice and Disparity at a Young Age

People came from the farms of rural Alabama to our area in search of work. Many saw Mobile as a metropolitan hub with more opportunity—but jobs were scarce or nonexistent.They came to Mobile, which was considered a metropolitan area with more opportunity, but living conditions varied greatly. Some families lived in public housing—what we called "The Projects."

Historically, during the 1940s and 1950s, following World War II and the Korean War, many of these housing projects were built across Mobile to accommodate the growing population and returning veterans.

Some of these housing projects became iconic landmarks, especially those located just outside of downtown. Their names will likely never be forgotten. Over time, many have been torn down—often without being replaced. In some cases, they simply vanished, leaving behind empty lots and erased histories.

Several public housing communities in Mobile once served as home to hundreds of families, but over the years, many were closed, demolished, or left to deteriorate—with little clarity on where the displaced residents went.

The Orange Grove projects, just north of downtown with nearly 800 units, endured significant damage from Hurricane Katrina in 2005. They were eventually demolished and replaced with a much smaller development now known as Renaissance Homes. The scale of the new housing left many wondering: where did all the original residents go? That question remains unanswered.

Roger Williams Homes on St. Stephens Road, which included 452 apartment units, was closed in 2016 and has since been completely wiped from the landscape. The buildings are gone, replaced by neatly kept grass and young trees—yet no sign remains of the people who once lived there.

The Josephine Allen Homes, also known as the Happy Hills community, included 292 residential units. After closing in 2011, the complex sat vacant for nearly a decade before being officially marked for demolition in 2020.

Two other longstanding communities—R.V. Taylor Projects and Thomas James Homes (commonly referred to as Birdville)—have been deemed beyond repair. Both are located in the area known as "Down the Bay" and have long been targeted by federal housing reform efforts. These closures are part of a broader national initiative to phase out public housing projects, but the human cost is often left unaddressed.

The loss of these homes reflects more than just changing infrastructure. It marks the disappearance of entire communities. In many cases, residents were displaced without a clear plan for relocation—leaving behind a lingering question: where did they all go?

Depending on who you ask, the exact boundaries of 'Down the Bay' changes. According to a January 12, 2023 University of South Alabama article by Rachel Hines, *Down the Bay: A Historic Mobile Neighborhood,* Down the Bay's boundaries are: North to Government Street, South to Baltimore Street.

Beyond the central neighborhoods near Mobile Bay, two of the most historically significant African American communities in Mobile are *The Bottom* and *The Campground.*

The Bottom, located just north of Dr. Martin Luther King Jr. Avenue (formerly Davis Avenue) and about a half-mile from downtown, was bounded by Three Mile Creek to the north and west. Its name came from its low-lying position near the creek bed. Developed in the late 19th century, The Bottom became the second African American community established in the area, soon after the formation of its neighboring district, The Campground.

The Campground Historic District, named after the Old Camp Ground—a Civil War military encampment—is another vital piece of Black Mobile's history. Bounded by Martin Luther King Jr. Avenue, Rylands Street, St. Stephens Road, and Ann Street, the Campground spans roughly 370 acres and includes 166 contributing buildings. Homes in this district range from shotgun to bungalow-style, dating from the late 19th to mid-20th century. In recognition of its significance, The Campground was added to the National Register of Historic Places on July 5, 2005. This neighborhood, like The Bottom, reflects the resilience, culture, and legacy of Mobile's Black community.

The Projects and other neighborhoods were carved out of the greater Mobile area specifically for people of color. In school, some kids wore designer clothes, and some didn't. The Lovetts never lived in the projects. I came to understand that there will always be poor people, but to see such an imbalance has always been troubling in my life. I saw people living in cardboard boxes. Other people came begging for salt, flour, and basic staples.That disparity in America has always troubled me. We're taught that this is the greatest country in the world, yet the gap between people—economically, socially, and racially—remains wide. Even over the six decades covered in this book, so little has truly changed.

Those realities shaped the path I chose in life. I learned to share, to value people regardless of their circumstances. Whether someone had money or not, they mattered to me. That belief runs deep in my veins, and I'll carry it with me for the rest of my days—until I reach my heavenly home.

Beyond economic differences, I also stood out in more personal ways. There were a few things that set me apart from the other boys in the neighborhood. For one, as far as I knew, I was the only one who had been born in a hospital. At that time, most Black children were delivered at home by a midwife.

Hospitals were segregated then—there were separate facilities for Black and white patients. I was born at Saint Martin de Porres, a hospital located in what is now known as Down the Bay. Dr. Oliver S. Gumbs delivered me, and I became the first boy in my neighborhood to be circumcised—a detail that made me feel even more different, even if I didn't fully understand why at the time.

In 1971, the African-American Heritage Trail of Mobile placed a marker at the site of the hospital. Saint Martin de Porres eventually closed following the desegregation of hospitals, which reduced the need for separate medical facilities for Black patients.This and other markers throughout the area were as a result of the historical markers project. With desegregation, the black folks' hospital closed and in 1976 became a nursing home – the Allen Memorial Home.

As far as I know, all of the boys born before 1952 were not circumcised. Once again, I was different. This affected my thoughts of manhood and created a phenomenon, especially when we walked around nude. After swimming, there was an obvious difference in the way our bodies looked when naked. The other boys walked around with an extra two inches on their penises called the foreskin. Penis size played a large part in a boy's confidence and self-esteem in our community. That plays into the motivation of a person and their goals.

Some men can find success by overcompensating for lack of size. Other men have natural confidence because they are well-endowed and feel good about themselves. They assume that they deserve what they get. I had to deal with a lot back then because of my disability and other issues. I felt special about my circumcision, and my size, so it had a positive impact on my confidence. That helped my motivation. Some of the guys in my neighborhood had low self-esteem because they were too small. That didn't run in my family. There have been men in politics and in the public eye who have been known to bring up the size of someone's hands just to make people think about penis size. The competition never stops!

I lived about five blocks from the Mobile River, which empties into the northern end of Mobile Bay. Several smaller rivers also flow into the bay, and Adams Street ran downhill toward the water and downtown Mobile. Just beyond that area lies Africatown—a place with deep historical roots and personal significance. My mother's baby sister is buried there, tying our family to this remarkable community.

Africatown was established by 32 West Africans who survived the last known illegal shipment of enslaved people to the United States in 1860. They arrived aboard the Clotilda, a ship smuggled into Mobile by a local shipbuilder who made a bet that he could bring in Africans without being caught. Although the U.S. had banned the transatlantic slave trade in 1808, the Clotilda carried 110 men, women, and children from what is now Benin. To hide evidence, the ship was deliberately sunk. In January 2018, remnants of a ship emerged from the mud after a storm; by May 22, 2019, researchers confirmed it was indeed the Clotilda. That discovery brought national attention to Africatown—also known as Plateau—which is now recognized as a national landmark. I imagine the conversations among descendants must be rich and powerful, knowing the world is finally acknowledging their story.

I liked hanging out in this part of Mobile Bay back then. It was a lot of fun swimming with the guys from the neighborhood. Despite the fun, the waters held hidden dangers.

One day, while we were enjoying ourselves, I suddenly found myself slipping beneath the surface. I couldn't swim my way up. The water was dark, and I lost all sense of direction. I couldn't tell which way was up—and I couldn't breathe. It was the first time in my life I realized I could die.

A friend, Mullins, had drowned in that same area, and the memory haunted my thoughts as the water filled my lungs. In those terrifying two minutes, drifting in the darkness without oxygen, I came to understand how fragile life really is. It nearly ended for me that day—just another afternoon with friends down at Mobile Bay.

Near-death experiences have a way of accelerating maturity. After nearly drowning in Mobile Bay, something shifted in me. The fear, the helplessness, and the realization that life could end in an instant stayed with me. From that moment on, I saw the world differently—more seriously, more urgently. That experience didn't just shake me; it changed me. My chronological age and mental age definitely changed at this moment.

CHAPTER 6

Where the Stars Slept and the Sausages Sold

Chitlin' Circuit Stories of My Youth

Sam Tunstall, a Black motel owner, built and owned a motel on the other side of the field behind our home.Mr. Tunstall was a smart, brown-skinned man who worked hard during the week and was very well-dressed on Sundays. He had a ready smile and I looked up to him. The Tunstall Motel was not an air-conditioned motel, but it was a well-built motel. At that time, African-Americans didn't have hotels or motels where they could stay. There were lots of dogs on Tunstall's property, and he liked to go hunting. The dogs were also a way to keep people from randomly roaming on his property. He built a rooming house for transients next to the motel. He was a real estate developer and a deacon at Sweet Pilgrim Baptist Church. Mr. Tunstall and his wife Viola were well-known around town. Truevine Missionary Baptist bought land that Mr. Tunstall owned. It's the location where Truevine is today.

Living behind the Tunstall Motel, I got a chance to meet all kinds of celebrities. They traveled all over the country, where they were welcome to sing, dance, and perform for white folks. But those same people couldn't walk through the front door, mingle with them, or even eat in the same room. I was very young, about 8 or 9 years old, and I didn't understand how the cruelty of racism kept these famous (and not so famous) men and women from living in a dignified manner. They take their talents on the road, from city to city. The road is not an easy life for anyone, especially in that era. They weren't allowed to stay where they wanted, at least, not anywhere that white people were staying. It's great that there were people who received the bands in their rooming houses all over the South. Entertainers who lived on the road had a place to be accepted. Musicians on the 'chitlin circuit', baseball players, and all varieties of exciting people came to Mobile to perform. I met people who were black music royalty. It was exciting, and it happened in my backyard, less than ten feet away from our fence. There was a rooming house in every major city for black people. In the city of Mobile, Tunstall Motel was the place to be.

Mobile, also, had the distinction of having another motel where famous people would stay. Both the LaGrand Motel and the Seaman's Club have been documented in the *Negro Traveler's Green Book.* The Green Book was created by a New York postman who had encountered racism as he did his job. Victor H. Green decided to create and publish annually a guide book for black people to find safe places to eat, sleep and get gas in the United States. Necessity is the mother of invention, after all. The LaGrand also catered to many rising stars. I had a chance to meet singers like Sam Cooke, B.B. King, Jackie Wilson, Howling Wolf, Aretha Franklin, Tyrone Davis, Joe Tex and the Revues, James Brown's band and so many more. They would stay at the motel with their bands, and there were always sounds of a grand party. The guests would be drinking and carrying on. I would imagine being one of the famous people having a fun time. Some of the windows of the hotel faced my backyard. There were heavy curtains on the windows, so I couldn't really see inside, but sometimes there were gaps in the curtains and I could get just enough of a peek from my bedroom window to make my young imagination go wild. Mainly, I would listen, and I could hear the men and women making noises inside the rooms. They might as well have been right in my backyard. I was just a little kid, so I had no idea what was going on. I didn't know that they were having sex. I didn't know what sex was or that sex was like that. It seemed like they were hollering. Maybe I assumed that someone was in trouble and that I needed to get help. Who knows what was going through my mind? What I witnessed, looking through those windows, prevented me from making a move. There seemed to be something important going on. I didn't know what it was. I only knew that I could hear the noises coming from the windows, and it fascinated me. I was a Peeping Tom who couldn't always see what was happening, but I could hear.

It was not a hotel or motel, but I would be remiss if I did not mention the International Longshoremen's Association Hall. The International Longshoremen's Association (ILA) Hall is a historic labor union meeting hall that was established in 1936, in order to represent the city's African American longshoremen. The hall was built in 1949. Many prominent African-American entertainers performed in its auditorium, just as they did in the motels and hotels. ILA Hall 1410 also became a gathering place during the Civil Rights Movement and on January 1, 1959, at Mobile's annual Emancipation Day program, it became the only place in Mobile to host a speaking engagement by Rev. Martin Luther King Jr.

Of course, there is a story that goes along with that bit of revelation. Some say that a group of religious leaders would not sanction a meeting and speech in our city by Rev. King. For many in this state and others, Mobile, AL was seen as a place where civil unrest did not raise its ugly head and, undoubtedly, they wanted it to stay that way. Exactly what would it look like for the non-violent, social activist (which was the Rev. M. L. King, Jr.) to ring in the New Year with others who might want to challenge the status quo? It seems the local Southern Christian Leadership Conference (SCLC) disagreed with the position taken by those ministers and made it possible for the Rev. M.L.K. Jr., to speak in the International Long Shoremen's Association Hall. The hall was added to the National Register of Historic Places on June 27, 2011.

One of those same SCLC members was also a deacon at Mt. Pleasant Baptist Church, where my grandfather, Rev. B.M. Lovett, served as pastor. Deacon Cleveland Alexander Wolfe's 16th child, Rev. Andrew Gregory Wolfe—a proud 1970 graduate of Central High School—recalls a powerful story from that time.

He tells of the speech delivered at I.L.A. 1410 Hall and the moment a brick was thrown afterward, striking his father in the chest. Fortunately, Deacon Wolfe worked as a winch operator on the Alabama State Docks and was wearing thick, protective clothing. His heavy-duty jacket likely prevented more serious injury. His wife, Irma Pearson Wolfe, reportedly held him and prayed over him in the aftermath.

There were no official reports of violence during the speech itself, and several African-American officers were present to help maintain order. According to oral history, some Black policemen even called in "sick" that day so they could serve as security for Dr. King.

This stands in stark contrast to Mobile's reputation at the time as a place largely untouched by civil disobedience or racial conflict. Yet, the hand that threw the brick was said to belong to a known member of the Ku Klux Klan—a reminder that beneath the surface, tensions were very real.

To gain a clearer and more complete picture of Mobile and its role in the Civil Rights movement, I encourage you to explore these stories for yourself. Mobile holds far more than meets the eye—countless families with rich histories have helped shape the fabric of the American South and the nation as a whole.

Sometimes, like a quilt that doesn't quite fit, history must be taken apart, re-stitched, and reassembled to reveal the fuller truth.

Miss Willie Mae Ford owned the Baby Doll Café next door to my grandmother Afrey's house. Our home sat right beside hers. Miss Willie Mae was known for her great sandwiches and served some of the best fried fish and chicken in the neighborhood.

Even as a child, I sensed there might be a way to earn money from the crowds visiting the nearby motel. It was obvious—even to me—that whatever was going on inside those rooms required a lot of energy. I figured that once the noise quieted down, someone inside would be hungry or thirsty. So, I came up with a plan.

I went to Miss Willie Mae and asked for several hot sausage sandwiches and soft drinks. I didn't have the money upfront, but she trusted me to bring it back. I returned to the motel and, slipping unnoticed through the halls, listened at the doors. If the room was quiet, I knocked. When someone answered, I'd offer them a hot sausage sandwich and an ice-cold Coca-Cola.

After all that "exercise," the guests were more than happy to enjoy a snack without having to leave their rooms. And just like that, I found a way to turn opportunity into a few dollars of my own.

Miss Willie Mae trusted me, so I went straight back to her café with the money. There were no credit cards back then, but without realizing it, I had started my own little line of credit with her. She let me take sandwiches and drinks up front, and I always brought the money back after making my rounds.

I saved up tip money from those sales and kept it quiet. My parents didn't know anything about it. After one particularly successful weekend, my grandmother asked, "Boy, where did you get all that money from?" I told her I was selling hot sausage sandwiches—but I kept the rest of the story to myself. No one knew where I was finding my customers.

CHAPTER 7

The Bell That Interrupted MLK

The Day Civil Rights Captured My Heart

In our home, we were taught to thank God regularly and to pray before meals. We held prayer meetings every Wednesday, and nightly prayers were part of our routine. My parents believed in the importance of faith, but their approach was more structured and moderate compared to some others in the community. Even with that difference, they instilled in us a lasting belief that prayer mattered. To this day, I still believe in giving thanks for everything I receive from God.

We had many interesting families in our neighborhood. Behind our house lived the Joe Jordan family, members of State Street AME Church. Joe was four years older than me, and their two-story home—still standing today—is now a historic landmark. Down the street lived the Davis family, known for their many children and their music. They eventually became the gospel group known as the Davis Family. The Davises were deeply involved in Holiness traditions and held prayer meetings almost every day. As a child, I didn't fully understand their worship style. During services, people would begin shouting, moving with intensity as if overtaken by something powerful. It was unfamiliar to me, and at times confusing. Still, even though my family practiced differently, we respected their devotion and recognized that we all valued the power of prayer—just in different ways.

As I mentioned, my grandfather, Mose Lovett, was a deacon at Truevine Missionary Baptist Church. My father didn't go to church like the rest of them and would be considered the black sheep of the family. Despite that, my brothers and I got baptized when we were twelve. We accepted Jesus Christ as our Lord and Savior, and then we were submerged in the water. My great-grandfather, Rev. B. M. Lovett was much older by that time. Rev. I. U. Leigh was the assistant pastor, so he did the honors and was allowed to baptize me. My grandfather and Deacon Campbell (the praying deacon) assisted, too. Deacon Campbell thanked God for everything. His prayers lasted anywhere from fifteen minutes to an Hour! He was an inspiration to me. I never realized how much God can do and how much He runs my life until I heard all of the things that Deacon Campbell thanked God for, and it taught me how to pray.

Selma University is an institution which was sponsored by the Baptist Churches all over the State of Alabama, including Truevine Missionary Baptist. They took up offerings at my church, and one of those offerings was for Selma University, which was located in Selma, Alabama. Sometimes they had four or five offerings in our church. The fifth Sunday was Youth Sunday. I was Junior Superintendent of the Sunday School during a quarterly visit to Selma University. The visits were made to determine what subject matters to teach. Our Sunday School teachers were required to go. I was young, so I made the trip with a few of the deacons. While I was there, the most important thing was going to happen at 10:30 a.m. That's when I was prepared to ring the bell that dismissed Sunday School. After that, I expected to get cookies and Kool Aid downstairs. That's how things worked at Truevine. Miss Johnson was a dietitian who worked for the schools and always had snacks for the kids who came to Sunday School.

That Sunday at Selma University, they said I rang a darn good bell. I was determined to get the Kool Aid and cookies that were waiting. At Selma University, they didn't tell me what time to ring the bell, but when I saw that it was 10:30 I rang that bell with great enthusiasm. The people laughed out loud. I wondered why they were laughing at me. All I did was ring the bell on time. I didn't even get the refreshments. Years later, someone explained that they were laughing because Dr. Martin Luther King, Jr. was the guest speaker at the time. It's hard to imagine that I had the privilege of interrupting him because I thought he was preventing the kids from getting Kool Aid and cookies. That's when I became aware of who he was, and I followed his legacy over the years as I became an adult. That bell ringing incident was my very first connection with Dr. King, and it launched the work that I did for him during my life. We all know how much he could talk, and he was going past his time. I wanted him to shut him up so I could get to the goodies.

CHAPTER 8

Merit Badges and Molestation

Truth Revealed in the Shadows of Time

Growing up in Mobile, we learned that the area we lived in was mostly African-American. Most of our friends and the people who cared for me were African-American. It was like a village, but when we went downtown to shop, things were different. We would go to Bienville Square, a historic city park located in the center of Mobile. That park was named after a Frenchman named Jean-Baptiste Le Moyne de Bienville, also known as Sieur de Bienville, Mobile's founding father. During that time in my life, segregation was in full force. They had one water fountain for whites and another one for coloreds. The whites only water fountain was refrigerated water, the colored water was not cold. Of course, the colored people couldn't drink from the white folk water fountain. However, I am proud to say that I slipped away and drank the white water from the white fountain every single chance I had! It made me feel like a human being. Other racist systems were in place to remind black people of their second-class status in the city. Black people went to places like Woolworth's and other eateries and had to watch white folks enjoying the convenience of going in the front door and enjoying their food, while we were forced to order our burgers and hot dogs from a back window. Everyone walked around like it was normal, as if it was supposed to be that way forever. When we would go on bus rides, I always wanted to sit in the front. I was fascinated with the drivers and how they handled such large vehicles. But we were deprived of the view from the front, so my parents would always lead us farther to the back of the bus. It made me even more aware of the racial divide. I hated being forced to sit in the back. It also happened when I was making all of those trips to the hospital early on for all of my various injuries. There was always something to remind me of the lack of status we held in the world. We even had theaters just for black people. There was the Ace Theatre, the Lincoln Theatre, and some others, like Harlem Theatre in Down the Bay Mobile. The Saenger Theatre was for the whites. Eventually, they integrated and let the black folks sit up top in the balcony. How very white of them to consider that as being integrated. Just the fact that we were looking at the movie at the same time, even though we were not allowed to sit where we wanted, was considered integration.

In my neighborhood, I noticed that the men who worked for the milk company and delivered milk to the house were all white. The vegetable men who came into the community to deliver fresh vegetables were all white. It was painful to see all the white people coming into the community and collecting money from black people. They were very friendly while they were filling their pockets with black people's money. The newspapermen were always white, too. Money was collected by whites, who always had their hands out, collecting money from the black people, but it was not working the other way around. White people were not giving up their dollars to increase income in my community. It was a constant reminder of racism in my world, and I always felt that there was something wrong with that.

I was still a little boy when a friendly, white guy, who lived on Congress Street, liked to ride around our neighborhood and pick up boys. They would go home with him and, when they came back, they were able to buy cookies and other delicious things. One day, I got into his car and took the ride around the corner with a few other boys. What seemed like an innocent ride turned out to be something far more disturbing.But his friendliness masked something much darker.The white man took us to his house and performed oral sex on us. Then he gave us some change so we would keep quiet about it. We never said anything about what went on behind those closed doors. And he wasn't the only one who preyed on us. Other men did the same thing. They would pass through the neighborhood and approach black boys. At the time, I didn't know what molestation was. I just knew that it was important enough for these men to pay for our silence. As kids, we were told the story of Emmett Till. It instilled fear in us and taught us to be extremely cautious. We were raised to never speak negatively about white people—doing so could cost us our lives. Speaking out carried the very real risk of being lynched or hanged.

My lesson from that experience was that parents need to always know about the activities of their children. I never discussed the molestation with my parents. They went to their graves without ever knowing an entire community of young people was affected. Being exposed to that type of abuse affected me mentally and made me realize that children are not always safe. We thought that we were in a good neighborhood, yet, there was widespread sexual abuse taking place.

When I was nine or ten, I was in a period where I was not as athletic as other kids. I did not get picked to play on teams. My friends were all older, and I couldn't keep up. At one point during that time, I hung out with a neighborhood kid whose mother owned the corner restaurant before Miss Willie Mae. The kid had gay tendencies. He liked to play house and bake mud cakes. My father noticed that while Britt and LaGrand were in the street playing ball with all the boys, I was hanging around with my neighbor playing with dolls and doing things that were considered too girly. That was a problem in my house. I can't go into detail but let's just say that a way was made for me to experience female companionship on a whole new level. I guess I learned my lesson, because after that, I didn't want to play with that kid anymore. I was interested in something better than that. I remember that my father bought me a ball which allowed me to control getting picked to play or not. The big boys would pick me so they could use my ball. Genius! The end result is I was separated from the 'possibly gay' friend and involved more in sports. If I was even thinking about being gay, there was a cure (?) for it, even though it meant putting an end to my friendship. During that time period, being gay was unacceptable. My interest was playing and not 'gender decision-making'. I saw no reason to avoid any other person because of their being gay or not. I felt it was important to respect all of my friends, even if they liked boys or girls. I liked girls. I never had any preference to like boys.

One of the things that differentiated me and my two brothers from other boys in our community is that my mother insisted that we become Boy Scouts. She wanted us to grow up to be good husbands, good fathers and good men. She thought that if she put us in good company, we could grow up to be whatever we wanted to be. I was in Cub Scout Troop 205 at Stone Street Baptist Church, a historic church in Mobile. My Cub Scout leader was a lady named Mrs. Madison, who taught us many things about life. We wore our Cub Scout uniforms and had an opportunity to march in the Mobile Area

Mardi Gras Association's Mammoth Parade, which was on the Monday before Fat Tuesday (Mardi Gras). The Mobile Area Mardi Gras Association (MAMGA) was previously named the Colored Carnival Association and was incorporated in 1938 under the trusteeship of professionals in the Mobile community - W. L. Russell, DDS, J.T. McKinnis, a local mortician, Sam Besteda, Jr., a local tailor and J.A. Franklin, MD of which the current Franklin Primary Health Clinics across the state are named.

Mardi Gras in Mobile started in 1703, one hundred and thirty-four years before New Orleans started in 1837. Each city has several weeks of parties, balls and coronations a couple of weeks before Fat Tuesday. In February, on Fat Tuesday there are other Mobile parades with white participants. We didn't really care that even the parades were separate. Our participation allowed us to see and be seen by the thousands of people who lined the streets. Later in life, I learned to see the value in those who were serving in the military and proudly wearing their uniforms. It was just outstanding as I achieved the status of Life Scout and was up for Eagle Scout. We had to obtain merit badges to qualify for that. I was in the Boy Scouts, in Troop 201, at Franklin Street Baptist Church. Our Scout Master was Donnie McCants. Mr. McCants owned a Shell Gas Station near my old high school. We were taught to do a good deed for other people each day. That was part of our motto. It stayed with me as I got older. I learned how important it was to be trustworthy, loyal, helpful, friendly, courteous, kind, obedient, cheerful, thrifty, brave, clean, and reverent to God.

We often went to a camp called Leon Roberts Camp. Camp Roberts was located north of Mobile, in an area called

Citronelle, AL. There is some documentation (a postcard picture according to Wikipedia) of swimming at the camp since the 1930's. Leon Roberts Camp was near a large lake that black Boy Scouts could swim in. While we were there, we learned new things about nature. I became interested in all types of trees. I learned how to tie a rope into different kinds of knots, like an eight knot. I had other important experiences, like learning to swim an entire mile, which was a big deal. Those are my positive lessons from the Boy Scouts. Unfortunately, there were also experiences in scouting that were tragic. Some of the people in charge of us were predators. They were responsible for giving us our merit badges. They were advisers who, at times, participated in molesting children. We wanted to get the merit badges, and they wanted to do a little licking on us. That is something that I'm sad to say happened. I'm not trying to tarnish the Boy Scouts. But the truth is that there were parents who trusted their children with these men, simply because they wore uniforms and represented some authority. It is worth repeating that parents must know who is watching their children. As I got older and was about to become an Eagle Scout, we were able to raise the flag for big football games at Ladd Memorial Stadium in Mobile. If I was the one to let the flag up, I could stay and watch the football game. At 13 or 14 years old, we would take our uniforms off because we thought the girls would think that we looked like young boys. That's why we would always have a change of clothes. It's one of the things that pulls a lot of boys out of scouting. They want to be attractive to the girls, who liked the guys who wore fancy clothes instead of the little kids in uniforms. As I grew older, I didn't want to be a Scout anymore. I did not become an Eagle Scout. What I wanted was to be more socially accepted by the girls. In our minds we thought that girls liked guys wearing stylish clothes more so than guys wearing a Boy Scout uniform.

CHAPTER 9

The Real MVP'S: Sheroes

The Women Who Shaped My World

Within the 'hood (my neighborhood), some of the kids went to school at Caldwell Elementary, which was out of the district. I attended a school called A. F. Owens Annex School, also known as Clark. It was in downtown Mobile. The back of the school was on Joachim Street, and the main entrance was on Conception St., between Congress Street and Adams Street. It was in a very historical area of Mobile, now known as De Tonti Square. A. F. Owens School was the main building. The principal's name was Professor William Douglass Robbins, who served from 1932 until his death in 1963. He was another Hero of mine. According to the Mobile County Schools website, Professor Robbins came to Mobile with his family at the age of two. He graduated from the Broad Street Academy in 1913 and served his country during World War I. He had the privilege of receiving a secondary education and attended Alabama State College. Later, he received his Master's Degree from New York University. Those are just a few of his accolades. He brought his expertise into the teaching arena, where he shared his skills at several schools. In 1932, they built a new A. F. Owens School. Professor Robbins became the principal and ran an obedient school. He was a great advocate of respect among his students. The lessons remained in the hearts of his students, and we took them into our lives and careers. It greatly influenced our successes.

For years, most of the African-American students from Davis Avenue area, all around through the Bottom, the

Dump, and the Campground, attended A. F. Owens School under Professor Robbins.

I've told you about every neighborhood in the Mobile area except "the Dump". The very name should speak for itself. Believe it or not, the state of Alabama was once considered the dumping ground for the country because waste (yes, human too) was transported by trains into landfills from as far as 1,000 plus miles away. The landfills were located in poor neighborhoods exposing people of color to foul odors, insects, vermin, disease and an overall horrific standard of living. A 2019 article in '*The Guardian*' titled *'We're not a dump'* by Oliver Milman of Selma, Alabama shed light on the fact that waste was imported from across the country to West Jefferson County, Alabama on what was known as *"the poop train".* In West Jefferson County, Alabama, northwest of Birmingham and north of Mobile there was a landfill named Big Sky Environmental which was permitted to accept waste from 48 states, including New York and New Jersey. The county seat, spurred on by the outrage from the community, barred the landfill operators from using the rail spur connector to deliver waste materials. Rail cars started backing up near small neighboring towns. Intense national media attention caused New York and New Jersey to cease their poop trains. Around that time, there were 173 operational landfills in the state. The current number is 43, according to the Landfill Methane Outreach Program (LMOP), as of July 2023. Despite the decreased number, the plight of poor people in neighborhoods where toxic wastes are dumped has not significantly improved.

It is estimated that over 15 million people, worldwide, live and work on a garbage dump today. In Mobile, we had poor, vulnerable and disenfranchised people living on *'The Dump'*. The Hickory Street Landfill (*'The Dump')* was located at the intersection of Hickory & Chinquapin Streets in Mobile, AL. and, yes, people lived there. The Environmental Protection Agency (EPA) identifies certain sites because they pose or had posed at one time a potential risk to the health of humans and/or to the environment due to contamination by one or more hazardous wastes. These sites require a process of long-term response actions that involve responsible parties and the community members in the process. The Hickory Street Landfill, along with two others in Mobile County, are currently identified as "Active Superfund" sites by the EPA's National Priorities List. I began to wonder if the inalienable right to "pursue happiness" was really possible on '*The Dump*'.

So, students from every corner of our neighborhoods attended A. F. Owens school under Professor Robbins. I was fortunate to have a mother who always attended the school PTA meetings. That was unique because many of the families in our community were not as involved in the school lives of their children. They functioned on the fringes of the right thing to do. My mother was a person who tried to break the cycle of non-involvement and dysfunction in our own family, which was hard to do, but still became her mission. To their credit, the students' families helped each other in any way that they could. They would lend a hand, share information, borrow and loan that cup of sugar – anything to help a neighbor. Therefore, I knew all the neighbors, unlike how it is in today's communities.

I had a principal named Annie Crockett. She was loved and respected by all of the parents because she was good at enforcing the rules. She, like so many others, rose to the occasion. She was my '*She-ro*'. The students thought she was good at robbing us of our joy. Mrs. Richardson was my 1st grade teacher. She was nice and very tall. I had already learned cursive writing in pre-school from Mrs. Love at Josephine Allen Institute. Then Mrs. Richardson (yes, another Shero) had to go back and teach me to print my letters. My 2nd grade teacher was named Agnes Scott. She was a beautiful, black woman who treated me very special, and was so fair-skinned that she almost looked white. She motivated me and was my mentor until she passed away several years ago. All of these women in my early school years were important in my life – every one of them a Shero.

My favorite teacher was Connie Davis. She taught 3rd grade. I was an impressionable boy, and she made a strong impression on me. She heard of my reputation as a great student. One day, she took a poem that we did and entered our entire class into a contest at a local radio station with it. I was given a chance to recite the poem on the air. It was called "The March Wind" by Edwin Ford Piper.

The March Wind
by Edwin Ford Piper

The March wind rushes with a shout across our little town. It turns umbrellas inside out and makes the people frown. Loose papers sail down the street. All the children laugh and play. There's nothing that can beat this wind, which is so gay. ~

It was amazing to go home and wait, and then suddenly hear

my voice on the radio. It's like a recording artist who records a song, and then one day they hear it and say, "Hey, that's our song. They're playing it on the radio!" My family rejoiced with great laughter and pride. It was an opportunity to shine that made me feel like I was famous. I felt that I had done something outstanding and great, and something that no one else could do. It was the best confidence boost that I enjoyed up to that time. That feeling of power was strong, and it carried me a long way down the road of my life. I was only in the 3rd grade, but I'll never forget that feeling. I managed to find a way to be on the radio, even though I couldn't sing well. It was an amazing thing and I wanted to do something special to reward Miss Davis for giving me that opportunity. I fell in love with her in the process, and she promised me that when I grew up, she would marry me. So I would go home and eat all of my food so I could grow up faster. I couldn't wait to get older so that I could marry Connie Davis. She would even let me carry her books to the car. That put the biggest smile on my face and made me happy. She eagerly shared lunch with me, and I made sure to share my cake with her because I was in love!

One day, a guy in an Army uniform came to the school to see Miss Davis. His name was Mr. John Lily and she allowed him to carry her books to the car, instead of me. I felt very hurt, emotionally crushed. There is no underestimating the power of a boy's first love. A man came and took my place with the girl that I loved. What was I to do? I had not gotten older but I had not gotten any bigger. I experienced my first heartbreak and had to simply move on. I still owe her a lot. Because of her, I had my first time performing on the radio, my first time falling in love, and my first broken heart. I'd say that she had an unforgettable influence on my life. These days, I'm happy to know that Connie Davis Lily, my Shero and first love, became one of the best teachers in the Mobile Public School System. Mr. John Lily, the guy who wore the Army uniform and carried her books, is the man that she married. Mr. Lily became a great bandleader in the city of Mobile, and he became a Kappa Alpha Psi member and Hero to me. May they rest in peace. He was a great man, and I cherished them both. They have both died-one day apart. They had a combined funeral service and I was honored to be able to speak at their last services. I spoke and told the world this same story about the lady who so impacted my life - her husband too.

Alma Moore, who was my 4th grade teacher, used to send me to the store to get her a sausage sandwich. Yep, another Shero! She taught history. It was through her that I discovered that a person could travel the world through books. I read about Hank Aaron, the New York Yankees, Satchel Paige and Willie Mays. I loved books, and I loved being able to read. Most of the stories that I read were about people and things that were foreign to my world, but there was still a connection. Reading gave me things to dream about, goals to strive for, and food for my imagination. Reading changed my life.

In 5th grade, my homeroom teacher was Mrs. Dora Martin. She taught me times tables and inspired me to do poetry. I recited a poem by Edgar A. Guest. His poems were very inspirational and showed the upside of everyday life in a way that was very appealing to me.

It Couldn't Be Done by Edgar A Guest

Somebody said that it couldn't be done

But he with a chuckle replied

That "maybe it couldn't," but he would be one

Who wouldn't say so till he'd tried.

So he buckled right in with the trace of a grin

On his face. If he worried he hid it.

He started to sing as he tackled the thing

That couldn't be done, and he did it!

Somebody scoffed: "Oh, you'll never do that;

At least no one ever has done it;"

But he took off his coat and he took off his hat

And the first thing we knew he'd begun it.

With a lift of his chin and a bit of a grin,

Without any doubting or quiddit,

He started to sing as he tackled the thing

That couldn't be done, and he did it.

There are thousands to tell you it cannot be done,

There are thousands to prophesy failure,

There are thousands to point out to you one by one,

The dangers that wait to assail you.

But just buckle in with a bit of a grin,

Just take off your coat and go to it;

Just start in to sing as you tackle the thing

That "can-not be done," and you'll do it. ~ **poetryfoundation.org**

I can still recite that poem to this very day and you know she was my Shero!

When I attended Dunbar Jr. High School, grades 7 thru 9, another teacher, Miss Stallworth, put me in a science fair. I was more of a geek than a jock. I didn't go to many of the games at school. The jocks were only trying to get the girls. Strangely enough, I put all of my time into practicing to make the team! I became a first-team starter as a shooting guard. I was a good student and always got A's and B's on my report card. There was a lot to be said for a boy who could put his thoughts into words. There were plenty of girls who appreciated that. I accomplished a lot more after being able to recite a poem on the radio for Miss Connie Davis. I became very well-read in English. Now, because I was a good academic student, I placed high in science, qualifying to represent Dunbar at the science fair and Ms. Stallworth would not release me to go play in the basketball games! I had to do experiments like measuring the effect of Carbon 14 on hamsters! The time it took for me to watch these experiments kept me out of the basketball games.

One of the experiences where I was able to use my knowledge is when I had an opportunity to read the newspaper as entertainment. Many men in the neighborhood faked being educated by buying a daily paper and sticking it in their pocket. They could not read and could not write, but they bought a newspaper every day. Sometimes people are insecure and do whatever is necessary to feel better about themselves and their situations. There's something about being fake that gets old, especially if your situation never improves. I was able to bridge the gap between the readers and the fakers. It didn't matter if they could read or not. No one cared. The way I read to them was interesting. I entertained them and educated them at the same time.

The two newspapers were The Mobile Press-Register, and the black-owned Mobile Beacon, owned by

the Thomas family. The Mobile Press-Register had a sports section, and I read articles and statistics to the men who gathered around a neighborhood tree to play dominoes. Men also gathered over by the Red Dot Cafe, which was owned by my Uncle Frank Lovett. It was located on Lipscomb Street and Joachim Street, near the fire station by downtown Mobile. That location is now gone, tree included. I would read about our local hero, Hank Aaron, who went to Central High School, which was the largest black high school in Mobile. Hank took his great talent and left Mobile to become a major league baseball player. I have an uncle, Winston Perkins, who would play ball with Hank Aaron – the big opportunity went to Hank. The armed services got Winston. We also kept up with Jackie Robinson and what he was doing with the Brooklyn Dodgers and what he was going through as he broke the color barrier. Another local hero was Satchel Paige, and there was a local Minor League Baseball team named the Mobile Bears. I would read about actor Chuck Connors, who played The Rifleman on television and was also a baseball player. We learned the difference between the National League and the American League. We liked the National League. They had players who were black.

I need to give you a little history lesson on those heroes who reported the news in our community. The *Mobile Beacon* was the longest published, family-owned and oldest African-American newspaper in the state of Alabama, from 1952 to 2019. There is a storied history behind the Mobile Beacon. One of the forerunners of the Beacon was The Alabama Citizen, founded in 1947 by Frank P. and Lancie Thomas in Tuscaloosa AL. The *Citizen* was published up until 1963. This was followed by the *Mobile Weekly Review* which became the *Mobile Beacon* in 1952. Frank P. Thomas, Jr. was a part of the history of desegregating the University of Alabama. Frank was a WWII vet who accompanied Arthurine Lucy to the University of Alabama in Tuscaloosa. Arthurine Lucy was an American activist who is credited with being the first student of color to attend the University of Alabama. Ms. Lucy began her quest to attend the University of Alabama in 1952 but would not have her first class until 1956 when she entered the graduate library science program. Both Frank P. and Lancie Thomas were activists who, since that time, have been honored in the National Hall of Honors for the National Newspapers Publishers Association and the Alabama Press Association. The Publisher/CEO of the *Mobile Beacon*, Cleretta Arizana Thomas-Blackmon learned the newspaper business at the feet of her parents - Frank and Lancie

Thomas. In 2018, Ms. Thomas-Blackmon announced that the newspaper would close, due to her advanced age, health concerns and not having anyone else to take over the paper. The last publication of the *Beacon* was a 2019, 32nd edition, January 2 – 8, 2019, 75th volume of the paper. A long and distinguished run of a much-needed paper that catered to the members of our community. Cleretta Arzinia Thomas-Blackmon died in 2022 – a legend and a Shero.

The University of Alabama would have yet another significant event to occur in the annals of Alabama's civil rights history. On June 11, 1963, George Wallace, then Governor of Alabama, stood in front of Foster Auditorium at the University of Alabama in Tuscaloosa, Alabama, in a symbolic attempt to block the entry of two African American students, Vivian Malone from Mobile, AL. and James Alexander Hood from Gadsden, Al., and stop the desegregation of schools. It is accepted that Wallace's inaugural promise of "segregation now, segregation tomorrow, segregation forever" was the primary and driving force behind his actions. That incident became known as the 'Stand in the Schoolhouse Door' and, to this day, is recognized as a seminal event in the course of the Civil Rights Movement in the State of Alabama.

As it happened, bringing the news to others was one of my earliest spotlight experiences. I achieved status by reading to these men, and I became a trustworthy favorite to them. They felt important when they sent for me. They didn't send for my brothers. They sent for me, and it gave me a great sense of accomplishment. Even at the age of ten, it gave me a sense of knowing my value and where my place could be in the world. I felt important, all because I could read.

Something else happened when I was in 5th grade. There was talk about bringing a battleship to Mobile, Alabama. A person was able to place a coin or two into a collection box. A dime or a nickel was enough. The city wanted to bring the Battleship Alabama to town, and we made it happen, because it now sits on the causeway between Mobile County and Baldwin County in the heart of Mobile Bay. The battleship made us proud and became the most popular tourist attraction in Mobile. During that time, President John F. Kennedy was in office. They said that Communism was coming to attack our country and that Cuban dictator Fidel Castro was the person who was going to do it. In Cuba, The Bay of Pigs effort to overthrow Castro had failed. All of this led to the Cuban Missile Crisis. In class, we had to practice running to the closet or going under the desks because of a foreign enemy, which was Cuba. That was the first time we learned that war could take our lives, and we were taught to do what we needed to do to survive. Later, we learned that a heroic President Kennedy had turned that situation around. This enabled us to learn the importance of foreign affairs. Countries outside of America could come and destroy us, and we were right in the line of fire. It made our world bigger. We realized that life was more than our street, our neighborhood, the community around us, our city, or even our country. We learned to be more conscientious.

One day during my 6th grade class, some students were allowed to leave school. It was a rare privilege. Brenda Kennedy (married name is July) went to the store to buy Haas-Davis sausages for the teachers. They were the best sausages in the city of Mobile. When she returned, she told us the saddest news I could have imagined. She had found out that President John F. Kennedy had been shot and killed in Dallas. On that day, she was a messenger and a Shero. We all cried, even though we didn't know him personally, because he represented the leadership of our country and he was a special man – a hero. It was the first time in my life that I felt a bond with my country, with the people of the United States of America. We, as black people, had been treated so mean and cruel in America. JFK was our leader, fighting against the hardships and negativity. He was our beacon of light, shining through the darkness of segregation in our lives. It was a darkness that attempted to destroy black people. President Kennedy wanted to liberate us from that terrible condition. The kids I grew up with had an awareness of feeling less-than, even at that young age. I already believed that we were different from the white people in our community. With President Kennedy's death, we felt as though we experienced a setback to our freedom here in America.

I was also in the 6th grade when the Mobile Public Library had a reading contest. My family didn't always have money to take vacations, so my mother allowed me to join a reading contest at the library. The Davis Avenue Branch of Mobile Public Library was built in 1931 in the racially segregated City of Mobile specifically to keep the races as separate in their library experiences as they were in their schools. Black people were prohibited from using the libraries designated for 'whites only', so this much smaller 'branch' was built for Negroes/Coloreds. Local African-Americans in the community are said to have helped collect used books for the library and to raise money for purchasing new books. In 1956, the first African American to hold a Masters Degree in Library

Science, Virginia Augusta Dillard Smith, was hired as the Head Librarian for the Mobile Public Library Davis Avenue Branch. Ms. Smith also held the distinction of being the first fully credentialed Black librarian in the State of

Alabama. She is said to have been the first to initiate the Dr. Martin Luther King Jr. celebration in the City of Mobile. She was hired as Head Librarian of the Toulminville Branch Library in 1961. The Mobile Public Library Davis Avenue Branch 3-room facility was enlarged a bit in 1961. With desegregation and the civil rights legislation of the late 60's, the library was used as a repository for government documents. Ms. Dillard-Smith remained at the Toulminville Branch until she retired in 1987, after giving more than thirty years of service. She was considered a 'Servant and Leader' of people, as well as my 'Shero'. In 1983, the branch library was listed on the National Register of Historic Places. Currently named The National African American Archives (on Martin Luther King Avenue), the building serves as a repository for documents, records, photographs, books, African carvings, furniture, and special collections that relate to the experiences of African Americans in the city of Mobile, state of Alabama and the United States of America. The name came from a community group founded by Mobilian, Delores S. Dees, that got the city to lease the building to them in 1992. Ms. Dees was the first president and executive director of the group which was able to expand and add 'and Multicultural Museum' to the title. In 2023, it was named 'The Historic Avenue Cultural Center'.

The Davis Avenue Branch library facility may have been small, but the contest itself was huge! I had a chance to read 75 books in one summer! I found out that you can go back into the past, learn about what has happened before, and be inspired and enlightened by people who have been dead for a very long time. I learned stories about great people like Frederick Douglass, Daniel Boone, George Washington, Thomas Jefferson, Benjamin Banneker, George Armstrong Custer, Helen Keller, Benjamin Franklin, and other people who had done great things in their lives. By reading books, I learned about Native Americans and the cruel and unfair treatment they received. There were stories about athletes like Mobile-native Satchel Paige and other members of the Negro Baseball League. There were books on the Civil War and slavery – both are sad footnotes to the birth and life of our nation.

The more I read, the more I wanted to read. I continued to search for more knowledge. I needed to know more about the slave trades. I found that today there is a free online Trans-Atlantic Slave Trade Database that provides detailed data on 36,000 trans-Atlantic slave voyages. That database is said to be the result of about 40 years of archival research and is housed at Emory University. I took a look at some information about the Clotilde to get a sense of what may have happened on that schooner. The Clotilde was a two-masted schooner with a deep hull and was designed for the lumber trade. At 86 feet long and 23 feet at its widest point (the beam), the cargo hold was reported to be big enough to hold 120 tons of cargo. If each person (yes, they were people) weighed about 165 pounds and had about 4 cubic feet of space, then the space could potentially hold roughly 2, 500 people. We really don't know the exact dimensions of the Clotilde's cargo hold so we are guesstimating. We do have information thru the National

Archives at Atlanta, that the swift schooner initially built to haul lumber entered Mobile Bay on July 7, 1860 carrying "103 slaves from a foreign kingdom, place, or country - more or less". Other sources have stated as many as 110 slaves. They were reportedly ranging in age from 5 to 23. You may be thinking that for a ship that could potentially hold so many people, the slaves on the Clotilde had roomy accommodations. But how many actually on-boarded the ship? How many chose a watery death overboard, instead of staying chained up and lined up sardine-style below the deck of the ship? The Clotilde is assumed to have had 4-5 cubic feet of space below deck. Slaves were placed in the ship's hold in spaces 16 inches wide and 3 feet tall. They did everything together – screaming, praying, crying, defecating, urinating, living and dying. How many were tossed overboard before the ship landed? The whole truth of this slave voyage and the many others that happened, despite slave-trading being outlawed in 1808, will never be known. From 1500 to 1866, 12.5 million Africans were captured, transported and enslaved. It's a sad truth we are forced to accept. A complete history can never be taught. Not because of 'cancel culture' or because anyone will feel shame at the telling of the tale. It's because the details are not complete, known, or cherished as they should be.

Books educated me. I learned about John Newton, the writer of the song *Amazing Grace*, who was himself the captain of a slave ship. The song was based on his own personal experience as a slave trader who had the responsibility of throwing dead bodies into the ocean. In his past, a violent storm created a near-death experience, inspiring him to convert to Christianity. His song was about redemption and forgiveness.

I learned so much about history that I wanted to become a historian. A lot of what I talk about in this book relates to history. It's important to know where you've been and not repeat mistakes as you move forward. History broadened my view of the world and showed me how to go to exotic and foreign places without physically being there. At that time, you couldn't Google information. You had to go to the library to get a book, and you had to know what section in the library to look for it. We had to learn the Dewey Decimal System. That helped me to prepare for high school and college, even though I was still in elementary school. I thank God for the opportunity to read 75 books in one summer. It was a challenge and a great experience which expanded my mind. It is so important to learn how to read. We've gotten away from that. People don't read newspapers anymore. People don't read books. I wonder who's going to read this book??? With computers and cellphones, we get a small part of the picture. Reading is critical and probably lead to my wonderful career. It can help each of us to dictate what type of life we want to live.

CHAPTER 10

The White Man's Ice Is Colder

The Painful Cost of Praise, Perception and Profit

Truevine Missionary Baptist Church had many deacons. I was proud of all of them. An early childhood friend, Sylvia, was in my Sunday School classes and helped me recall some of the names and situations from Truevine's past. We both remembered Deacon Campbell and his famously long prayers, and we had Deacon Grayson, with his analogies of various Old Testament and New Testament books.

Deacon Israel Packer, Sylvia's grandfather, was Superintendent of Truevine's Sunday School and a central figure in the community. He was president of the PTA at A. F. Owens Elementary School and he owned a business - the '*In the Bottom'* store located at Persimmon and Pecan streets. Deacon Packer was, also, the only African-American 'glass man' in Mobile. Anybody who needed car windows repaired would call on him. Between the time-honored car dealership in Mobile, *Joe Bullard Oldsmobile*, and others, it seemed to the family that Israel Packer was called every day! Deacon Packer had six children, 6 girls and 1 boy. One of his daughters was Sylvia's mom.

Deacon Eugene Antone had 14 children (8 boys and 6 girls), with Sylvia's mother, Julia. Deacon Antone was Vice-President of the AF Owens school PTA. Sylvia recalls that, while some members of her family were not particularly educated it was said that "they got things done". Mrs. Julia Antone lived to be 102 years old – over a century of dedicated service to her God, her family, her church and her community.

Deacon Joe Dotch and his wife, Mabel Powell Dotch, had 14 children. To say that the deacons of Truevine were prolific is, truly, an understatement. Those six parents with a good number of children always won the Mother's Day and Father's Day Awards in our church.

One of the deacons who impressed me was Deacon William Wiggins, who was a businessman. He was my grandmother's brother-in-law. Deacon Wiggins and his wife, Ruth, had 15 children. Deacon Wiggins was a local, young entrepreneur who owned a grocery store and a beauty parlor. The beauty parlor was where Ms. Irma Moore (Ms. T.) and Mama Jettie Mae held court and was on the corner of Persimmon and Plum Streets. One of Deacon Wiggins' daughters, Gloria, shared with me that her dad built a 10-room house with "nothing but a string". In that home on Persimmon Street, they had all of the conveniences - washer, dryer, flooring! Her dad was a visionary and a great disciplinarian.

When I wanted to get a job, I thought I had a chance to work with one of the trustees at Truevine, Mr. Smith, who owned an ice truck and distributed ice to the neighborhood. All of the people in the community who didn't have electric refrigerators had to buy ice to keep food cold. Fancy appliances existed for wealthy people, but they didn't exist for our community. So, every day Mr. Smith would come and deliver the ice. However, when I asked him, he would not give me a job. I think it was because of my leg braces and lack of strength. The job called for strong, muscular guys to lift the 25 lb. blocks of ice from the truck. But there was a white guy, who we called Mr. Charlie. He would let me and my friends ride on his truck while he distributed his ice to the community. Soon, Mr. Charlie began selling more ice because I got the word out that the white man's ice was colder than the black man's ice. He was making more money with me on his truck, and that created a problem.

My great-grandfather, B. M. Lovett, pastor at Truevine, saw that his trustee's contributions to the church were getting short because he wasn't making as much money. The news got back to the church that B. M. Lovett's great-grandson was working for Mr. Charlie and telling people not to buy Trustee Smith's ice. My great-grandfather had to put a stop to that. He hurt my feelings and forced me to quit. I was having a negative effect on Trustee Smith's family. I also jeopardized his livelihood and his standing in the community. As a result of working with Mr. Charlie, there was a very troubling period in the relationship I had with my great-grandfather. He was opposed to me having that job, even though I loved it and was good at it. I wasn't as strong as the other boys in the community, but I was able to tell people that Mr. Charlie's ice was colder, and they would buy it. Not because it was colder, but because I was saying that it was. I didn't know that I was a salesman at that point, but my natural abilities began to shine through, even way back then. I was excited because Mr. Charlie hired me, not for my physicality, but because I could sing the virtues of his ice out loud. I was using a natural gift that I enjoyed. Instead of being proud and encouraging me, the elder of the Lovett family was breaking my spirit with his disapproval.

After that, I went to work in the potato fields. There was a bus that picked up the men and boys in the neighborhood and took them to pick potatoes. They paid us three cents for every sack. On the first day, I learned the ropes. We could take as many breaks as we wanted to, and get snacks at the concession stand on credit. I got Vienna sausages, a coffee roll and a soda on each break. I owed them more money than I had made at the end of the day. That was my shortest job.

From my work as a little entrepreneur, I learned that it takes money to buy things. Our lives are centered around learning and developing an ability to create an income source. I found ways to do work that allowed me to afford things. I was good at performing tasks and doing things to get money, so that I could buy cookies, ice cream, and candy. I had to think like a businessman. You couldn't be a success without a back-up plan. You had to have money for when your parents said, "No, we don't have any money to give you." If you became complacent, you ended up with no money, while other kids had plenty of money. But if you got creative, you got what you needed. I asked my Grandma Afrey to be my banker. She helped me to save money and helped me to explore a world outside of my own. She died of a heart attack one Sunday morning while she was getting ready for church. Dr. Michael Scott, who was at Truevine when it happened, rushed over to the house and tried to revive her. I've always been grateful to him for his heroism in trying to save her, but she had lived a good life and it was her time. Still, it hurt me deeply when she died.

The first time I went outside of Mobile was when my mother gave me, Britt and LaGrand a train ride to Birmingham. I discovered other places were not the same as what I knew in the neighborhood. I was proud to see entrepreneurs come to the community. I liked watching the way that they handled their money. The milkman had a big wallet with a chain attached. It had all of his money in it and hung outside of his pocket so that he could fold dollars into it.

One day, Grandma Afrey took me on a train ride with her to visit her daughter and son-in-law in Rahway, New Jersey. My aunt Edith Lovett-Perkins and Uncle Winston Perkins were my father's sister and brother-in-law. I felt very grown-up because I had a wallet that hung out of my pocket, just like the milkman back home. On the train, I had a chance to see the Appalachian Mountains for the first time. It was significant to me because I saw geography, just like I had studied in school. I had never seen mountains in person before. During the trip, my aunt and uncle took us to New York City, I was in awe. I looked up at the tall buildings, even though people advised against it. They told me that looking up would draw unwanted attention to myself, labeling me as an outsider, a country hick and a victim waiting to be taken advantage of. Finally, we arrived in Coney Island, and I realized my wallet was gone. Somebody stole all of the money I had saved! It was a sad lesson to learn. Someone can take everything from you when you're not paying attention, so you have to protect yourself. So, don't wear a wallet that sticks out of your pocket. And if you visit New York City, especially if you've never been there before, don't look up!

When I was ten years old, My Uncle Frank Lovett, allowed me to come and clean up the Red Dot Cafe. I swept the floors and took out the trash. I was just a young kid and didn't have any skills, but he noticed that I read the newspaper to the guys who played dominoes and couldn't read. Many of the customers were longshoremen. Frank Lovett recognized my ability to communicate and draw a crowd. That enhanced his clientele and was good for business. He also noticed that many of these guys needed to go somewhere else to get their shoes shined, so he came up with the bright idea to put a shoeshine parlor on the front porch. There were three chairs where folks could sit and get their shoes shined. Uncle Frank told me that was going to be my first business, as the owner of a shoeshine parlor. There was one problem. I didn't know how to shine shoes. It didn't take me long to figure out that I had to find people who did know. If we were able to get fifteen cents for a shoeshine, then I would give a nickel to the guys that I hired, and I would take a dime. That was my plan. I found people who wanted a shoeshine and brought them to the cafe. But my guys didn't go for that, so the controversy continued. The boys kept debating about who was going to bring in the customers and who was going to shine. So, the business failed. I was too young to know how to manage all of that. The lesson I learned was that your business could fail if you couldn't control the pricing, or the personnel. It was quite interesting. I continued to sweep the floors and read the newspaper for free, but I lost my source of income and failed. If you open a business, you need to know as much as you can. You have to know your product and be able to do the job yourself if you have to. You can hire skilled people, but you should know as much as you can about it yourself. That knowledge that I gained as a boy was something of great value to me as I grew into an adult.

CHAPTER 11

Before the World Changed Us

What I Learned from Joey, John, and the Boys on the Block

Joey Lipscomb was my first white friend. A few white people still lived in our segregated community. Joey and I played in my yard together. Oscar Hugh Lipscomb, who was the first Archbishop of the Roman Catholic Archdiocese of Mobile, was one of his relatives. Joey's mother worked in the Mobile Police Department. She flashed her badge a lot and was probably clerical. She feared being surrounded by black people. I learned to know white people from Joey and his family. Joey and I had opinions, but the world we lived in did not agree with us. We loved each other. I learned that it was possible to love someone who didn't look just like me. It was an experience for me to find those things out by having Joey as my friend. As we got a little older, we got separated somehow. It was the adults who had a problem with our friendship, not us. That's common in our experiences as African-Americans in this country. Things in my world may have changed, but, for a time, Joey Lipscomb and I were best friends.

John David Tate was one of my first great friends. We grew up together from way back in nursery school. We lived one block from each other and competed in just about everything from 1st grade to 12th grade. One of my favorite childhood memories is from the time we shared in the 5th grade. John and I were in the same homeroom that year when John became the school's ice cream man. He knew his multiplication tables. The ice cream was all for 7 cents, so he became an expert. He sold popsicles, ice cream sandwiches, and more. Mrs. Dora Martin knew that there was some competition between the two of us. She provided challenges for us and put us up against each other in different ways, and it was fun. Some days John got the best of me, and sometimes I was able to beat him. I thought I was a good singer, but John said I couldn't carry a tune. We battled it out in school and after school, too. We were always competing. Somehow, I managed to sneak past him most times, often by just a point. There was a group of our friends who played ball in the streets on weekends. We played on a concrete basketball court. Most of the time, my brothers and I had to do our chores first. John Tate had sisters to do a lot of the chores in his household. No matter what the situation was, no one complained about a thing. We were just glad to get out. It was like freedom.

When I was in the 6th grade, Miss Agnes Scott, who was in charge of the ice cream, had me take over John's position as the school's ice cream man. I had other responsibilities, like selling Krispy Kreme donuts from class to class. I beat John out of his fun job, and I even beat him out of one of his girlfriends. I beat him out of everything, except football. John usually got me in the street with football. Since we didn't have a gym in those days, we played outside in the backyard or on the curb. We were all like family. I had my two brothers. John had two brothers and six sisters, and they all ate well. There was also a family who had a lot of pretty girls. John lived behind them, and I lived diagonally across from them. We liked to sit on the curb to watch them. Naturally, we ended up looking at the same girls. When I came sniffing around a girl John liked, he told me to back off. There was always friendly competition. We never had fights over anything. John was stronger and faster, and I was taller. They called me a "long-legged rascal." Every girl in a pretty dress was a target. We were both after them.

When I was twelve, everything changed between John and me. I didn't mind wearing short pants because I was on the basketball team. John was too thick for the shorts but, during gym class, he tore up the floor in his comfortable clothes. The coach wanted him to try out for the team, but he wasn't interested. John told me to go represent, so I did. My nickname was 'Oop Dog'. I blocked shots and pulled rebounds while John cheered me on. He yelled, "That's the way to go, my homie!" I played basketball well, but John felt that I was falling in love too much. Instead of practicing, I was taking girls to the movies. The Ace Theatre was a favorite place of mine, so I spent a lot of time there. For a quarter, I bought three movies and stayed there all day, buying popcorn and candy. That was a good thing to do. I was obsessed with going to see movies. I liked the Lincoln Theatre, too. I stopped at Babe's Hot Dogs on Hospital Street where I could buy a delicious hot dog for ten cents. They always had a long line at Babe's. I would get three hot dogs and John Tate would get two. I always had a little more money than he did. There was a reason why. I figured out a way to maximize my finances. I shared that information with my friends. I told them to buy the ten cent hot dogs and hide them, or they would end up paying twice as much in the theater.

Dunbar Junior High, grades 7th thru the 9th, is where all of the neighborhood kids went, and they had good competitive sports. That's where I met Arthur Mack. Arthur was a neighborhood boy who was a grade behind me. I was on the basketball team and was very popular. Fortunately, I was talented at a lot of things. We had a lot of basketball courts around the neighborhood, and I had skills but the best player around there was a guy named Britt Stallworth. Britt played every day! Arthur's basketball skills were lacking, but I always encouraged him and cheered him on during pick-up games. One time, I saw him on a game day and asked, "You gonna come root for me today"? Arthur looked up to me. To him I appeared to be larger than life. He replied, "Yeah, I'll be there." I was proud to have his support. I was even prouder, in later years, as I followed his career(s) and learned of the great successes in his life. You see, Arthur went on to graduate from both the 'Branch' (Bishop State Community College) and the University of South Alabama. He was a well-known and accomplished athlete in track and field. We must recognize and thank him for his service in the military that resulted in his receiving both awards and commendations. He, also, became a prolific freelance and sports writer with over three decades of articles submitted to various newspapers and magazines – he received awards there as well. I am proud of all that he accomplished.

Mr. James Kennedy was an 8th grade teacher coming out of the Air Force. He had served in the Air Force from 1955 to 1958 and began his career with the Mobile County Public School System. Mr. Kennedy had us stand on a line, but I had big feet that stuck out from everybody. John Tate said, "Man, you gotta put your toe on the line." I said, "If I put my toe on the line, I'll be way back there." Everybody laughed. We had a great time going to school. Much later in my life, Mr. Kennedy would gain full-fledged 'Hero' status. He made a tremendous impact on my time as a college student at the University of South Alabama (USA). More about that time at

USA later, when Dr. James Kennedy was a mentor and accomplished academician at the University. In fact, he became the first African American to head the University of South Alabama Art Department. Anyway, that 8th grade year was a good year, and it became better as we moved on to 9th grade. There was a contest for the school Kings and Queens. John and I both had an opportunity to be Kings, but we declined. We knew ALL the girls in school and were already popular with them. It was also a good basketball year for me. Neither one wanted or needed to stand out further.

In 10th grade, John Tate and I both went to Central High School – colors maroon and white, the Wildcats football team, the Marching 130! We thought we were all grown up! We both had new cars and our worlds quickly changed. John had a GTO, and I had a Dodge Dart with three shifts in the column. We took turns riding in each other's cars. We would go to The Riviera Club. It was a nightclub where we were too young to be, and where they shouldn't have let us in. The first time that we did get in, we went to sit in the corner. We were checking everything out, and you know we were up to no good. Right away, Mr. Smith came over and caught us. Told us we couldn't be in there. We said we just wanted to sit with a Cherry Coca Cola, but we each had a shot of gin hidden in our back pockets. Mr. Smith let us slide, but told us not to start anything or say anything that would get us caught up. We assured him that we were going to be on our best behavior. At one point, I went to put a quarter in the jukebox and then turned out the party with a fancy dance. People in the club enjoyed my antics. They urged me on and began rooting for me, so nobody was trying to kick us out of the club. John and I were charming and fun, and we were able to get away with a lot. After that night, the door was open to us. John said, “It was all thanks to Big Al, who helped us to talk our way in.”

In 11th grade, John was on the football team, and I was in the band. We didn’t see each other as much, mostly passed in the hallway. I always took the time to talk with him, though. We double-dated and went to the junior prom together. The ladies loved us, and we loved them. I have very fond memories of John. He was one of my best friends in life, my favorite, my Hero.

My brothers and I wanted to play music. My mother encouraged that activity over football because, as she said, “I didn’t want you broke up.” So, we all got instruments, and we all played in the band. I played trombone, Britt played alto horn and trumpet, and LaGrand played French horn. We were three brass guys, and we all were talented. When I finished Dunbar Junior High on my way to Central High School, I had a friend from Dunbar named Louis Orange. We were friends from the time we met at Dunbar, all the way through graduation from Central High. We were number #1 and #2 in a lot of things. We were close friends and enjoyed being in the Central High School Band with its one hundred and thirty members. Louis played the trumpet, bass horn and drums. I played the trombone in the biggest high school band in Mobile. That period of my life required a bit of decision-making. Would I be a football player and participate in sports, or would I play trombone in the band? It was the time in my adolescence where I had many choices. I could be a great athlete, a great musician, or a great student. As for Lewis, he continued with music later in his life. He received a music scholarship from Texas Southern University, but made the choice to play in the Marine Corps Band instead and to be a daddy.

Lamont Jones was another heroic childhood friend. He was seven years older than me, but we had many adventures together. I lived on Adams Street, and Lamont lived down the block on Claiborne Street. Our world consisted of a neighborhood that was in a four-block radius. There was Miss Willie Mae's Cafe on one corner. Miss Teresa's convenience store was across the street on another corner. The Odell Cafe was around the corner where there were often fights that resulted in bodily injuries, like stabbings. On the back side of my house was the Tunstall Hotel. Two blocks away was the Seaman Rooming House. Ships docked in Mobile Bay and the seamen and Merchant Marines came to stay there. The Mobile River was six blocks east. One block away was Mt. Gilead Baptist Church. I played hide and seek underneath the church with the neighborhood children. We had a lot of fun, and the adults had fun, too. In the back of Lamont's street, there was an area where folks gathered late at night. They sold white lightning, which was illegally-made alcohol commonly called moonshine and hooch. Then there was the spot where the adults played cards into the wee hours. Adults also placed bets with the local numbers man. My parents didn't play, but Lamont's parents and grandmother did.

Ronald Gibbs was another good childhood friend. In over fifty years of friendship, Ron has inspired me in many ways. As kids growing up, we competed to make money. We were enterprising and would do all kinds of things to make a buck. I was generous with my friends. There was some bad in each of us, but the good surely outweighed it. There was always light at the end of the tunnel. Miss Willie Mae helped us with our endeavors by allowing us to help her at the restaurant. Whoever got there first helped to take the groceries in and be the one to get paid. Ron would stop playing football or whatever he was doing, just to beat me to it. We were in the Boy Scouts together and liked to compete. I was the one who encouraged Ron to enter the Boy Scouts, and I was a born leader. I was civic minded, and I liked to inspire people. Friends thought I came from privilege because my Uncle Willie and Aunt Lillian Lovett ran the funeral home. Even so, I always looked out for others and tried to be compassionate. If I saw a need, I did whatever I could to help. I was a bit of a diplomat. I often chose to offer advice, and because of my ability to look at both sides, I was able to diffuse any situation. I never had a harsh word with any of my friends. That didn't mean that friendships were not challenged.

For instance, there was Jim Henry James, Jr., who was my fifth- grade classmate. He was one of my best friends, and we called him "Bubba Jim". His family owned some grocery stores in the black community. "Bubba Jim" brought good food for lunch. He had lettuce, tomatoes and a special sandwich spread on his sandwiches, not just regular mayonnaise or mustard. He would have two or three sandwiches just for himself. Our school didn't have a cafeteria, so the students brought lunch from home. My mother was a great cook, and she wanted us to have tasty sandwiches, too. She put something balanced in our lunch bags every day. After I came in from selling ice cream, I would go back to my class and sit in the back after the lesson had already started. I always shared my lunch with "Bubba Jim", letting him have half of my sandwich. He was happy to taste the delicious sandwiches that my mother made. And there was no reason to eat them by myself. I shared what I had with my friend. I decided that I wanted to be a 'giver'. It feels great, and it brings as much joy to the giver as to the receiver.

One day, I came into class hungry. Can't remember why I didn't have my lunch, but some circumstance had left me without food that day. Naturally, I asked my best friend, "Bubba Jim", if he had an extra sandwich because I didn't have my lunch that day. I knew that I could get anything I needed from "Bubba Jim". If he had an extra pen or sheet of paper, he would give it to me. This time it was food that I needed, and "Bubba Jim" had baloney sandwiches. So, I asked him if I could have one of his sandwiches, and "Bubba Jim" told me "No" because he only had two sandwiches. I thought I was mistaken, and that I had heard him wrong. But that wasn't the case, and it disturbed me. He said that if he had three sandwiches he would have given me one. With only two, he wasn't willing to share. I was his friend, and I always shared with him. I was hungry that day. The fact that he wouldn't help me affected me deeply. I realized that his true feelings about our friendship were not good – at least not when it came to his sandwiches. It tainted our entire relationship. I learned that there needs to be an equal balance in relationships, and it's not healthy when one person is a giver, and one is a taker. So, be mindful of what your expectations are in any of your relationships. Experiencing imbalance is one of the most troubling aspects of a relationship that people go through. Selfishness is one of the reasons for the break-up of friendships and marriages. That lesson taught me that I don't have to be selfish. I only need to remember how I felt when "Bubba Jim" let me go hungry, and that reminds me to show compassion. I felt that he was thoughtless at the time, but that one selfish act did not define our friendship. We moved on, and “Bubba Jim” is still one of my best friends in life.

CHAPTER 12

When Home Became the Battlefield

The Lovett's Don't Fold

When I was in the 10th grade at Central High School, my parents got divorced. They finally realized that they preferred to live without each other. Being divorced was not a good thing in our family, but we all decided to move on. Britt and LaGrand chose to live with my father. I didn't want my mother to feel like a failure, so I went to live with her. And, of course, I was her baby boy. The house we lived in was at the end of Pinetree Drive, in an area of Mobile called Toulminville. That area is now Gethsemane Cemetery, but the house we lived in was the last house on that street. Soon after that, my mother met and married a man named Jack Jackson after a short period of dating. He seemed to be a very Christian man. He wanted me to change my last name to Jackson, but I didn't want to. Once a Lovett, always a Lovett.

The neighborhood my mom chose had many distinguished people living there, including the Mitchell family. The Mitchell family lived across the street. Dr. Joseph Christopher Mitchell, Sr. a prominent educator, taught biology at predominantly black S. D. Bishop State Junior College - now Bishop State Community College. Bishop State Community College (BSCC) was founded in 1927 as the Mobile, Alabama extension of Alabama State College. Everybody called it "the Branch". It was a branch of Alabama State College that was organized in 1936 and is documented in Wikipedia as America's first state-supported educational institution for blacks. On June 21, 1981, Dr. Mitchell was selected to serve as interim president, upon the death of Pres. Sanford D. Bishop. Dr. Mitchell served in that capacity until September

1981, when Dr. Yvonne Kennedy was appointed as the second president. I am pleased to call one of Dr. Mitchell's sons, Joseph Mitchell, one of my dear friends. Joseph sought and was elected to the Alabama House of Representatives, District 103, from 1994 to 2014. True heroes in that family.

One night, my mother was arguing with Mr. Jackson. It was late, and the sound of their raised voices startled me out of my sleep. People can have arguments, and it's no big deal. That's what a lot of couples do. But this was on a whole other level. The situation got crazy, and I'm not exaggerating. My mother and her husband ended up in a struggle with a gun. Can you believe it? A gun! Suddenly, a shot rang out. Before I even had a chance to react, a bullet whizzed through the headboard of my bed. It was only through the grace of God that the bullet did not hit me. It was devastating, and very traumatic, and reminded me that I could lose my life in a split second, without any warning. I decided that I could no longer live with my mother and my stepfather, so I moved in with my father and my brothers on Texas Street down the Bay.

During that time, Britt was an honor student in the Central High School Class of '67 and wanted to go to Alabama State University (A. S. U.) in Montgomery, AL after he graduated. He played in the band at Central High and was also on the basketball team. My mother pushed him to join the ministry, but he was too good-looking and debonair for that. Early one morning, I rode with Britt and my mother to Montgomery so that he could go to the university to take his college entrance exam at A. S. U. Britt had been to a Jackie Wilson concert the night before, and had stayed up all night. He was driving my mother's 1967 Dodge Dart. She was in the passenger seat and I was sitting in the back. As we went through Brewton,

Alabama, about 85 miles northeast of Mobile, we hit a curve, and my brother lost control of the car. We crashed violently and I almost went through the windshield. My left arm and hand went through the glass first. My face was damaged, too. It was horrible. My mother took responsibility for the accident, and I was a mess. The doctors had to put plates in my hand to connect it back to my arm. I also had a punctured lung and was in pretty bad shape. They kept me in the University of South Alabama Medical Center (U. S. A. M. C.) hospital for a month. That hospital is a significant and growing part of the Toulminville community to this day.

How many times have I come close to losing my life? Once again, I realized that anything could happen at any time. It scared me to know that I could be doing everyday things, without a care in the world, and could die. While I was in the hospital, I had plenty of time to think about what happened, and I held some resentment against my brother for his part in the accident. Britt hung out late and partied the night before his exams with no sleep. The accident changed the course of my future and ended any thoughts of my being an athlete because I could no longer use my left arm and hand. Britt gave up his plans for college and went to Detroit to work in the auto industry. He also married his high school sweetheart, Eloise Watson.

LaGrand, who was in the Class of '69, became involved with the pro-black revolution. His interests led him to some of the Black Panthers like Bobby Seale and David Hilliard, which kept him on the wrong side of the law. He traveled to the largest cities in America to expand the scope of what the Black Panthers were doing to help black people. With all of the controversy and bad press, things were bound to take a turn for the worse. There was big trouble on the horizon for William LaGrand Lovett and he eventually ended up with a choice to go into the military or go to jail. LaGrand quit high school in his senior year and went into the Army Infantry and became a paratrooper. He was sent to Vietnam and was involved in several suicide missions, but somehow survived. He had information on both sides. He was eventually captured and became a P. O. W. The enemy tried to force him to talk by turning him into a heroin addict.

Upon hearing about LaGrand's capture, Britt took action. Like something out of an action movie, he joined the Marines to serve in Vietnam and find our brother. My mother said that he had the highest IQ out of 42 battalions and they made him Sergeant-at-Arms. Somehow, with the help of an angel from the Central Class of 1968, Britt found LaGrand! Britt was able to get LaGrand out of Vietnam, but when LaGrand came back, he was court-martialed and did time in Fort Leavenworth, Kansas. After doing his time, he wandered all over the country. He never returned to a productive life. In a set-up, he was ambushed and killed in Kansas City in 1996. Heroism takes many forms, as it did with my brothers. There are some American hero stories that were never told. We have lived to see many examples of how America did not take care of veterans, failed them in so many ways, and ruined their lives. I lived to see the love between the Lovett brothers – to join the service, not only for our country but to help each other.

Not long after that, I had another car accident and injured my right hand. I had to have surgery on that, too. While recovering, I was not able to drive, so I asked my good friend, Louis Orange, to drive me around in my Dodge Dart 3-speed. One day, LaGrand, Louis and I decided to take a road trip to New York City, where we had relatives. We were small-town boys trying to be grown and had a bright idea for us to practice drinking before we went. We wanted to be like the big boys. The goal was to look sophisticated, not like the country bumpkins that we were. New York City was the most sophisticated place that we could think of, so we were very excited to see the lights of the city. Before leaving, we drove around Mobile, figuring out what to do. Then it was time to get something to drink. We found a wino who was willing to get us a couple of bottles of wine. We gave him money, and he brought back Red Dagger wine, which was very strong, and only sold in state stores. We began drinking, and Louis drank too much. We went to see my cousin, Willie Mae Taylor. She lived at the family house on Plum Street. She helped us to settle down. As soon as she greeted us at the door, she realized what was going on. She didn't want the neighbors to see us drunk outside, so she brought us into the house. She took care of us, and my brother and I finally sobered up. Louis said he was okay, too. He thought he was ready, but he upchucked soon after getting in the car! Unfortunately, we never made it to the Big Apple.

I guess you could say that some of LaGrand's social activism was in my spirit too. At Central High School, my high school homeroom teacher was Joycelyn Franklin Finley, and she taught black history. The Franklin Primary Health Centers in Alabama are named after Joycelyn's father, Dr. James Alexander Franklin. Ms. Joycelyn Franklin invited me to be a youth speaker for the NOW (Neighborhood Organized Workers) Movement. That group had a turbulent past. Noble 'Bip' Beasley was a fierce civil-rights advocate and was president of NOW, in 1968 when the organization began picketing and boycotting Mobile businesses. Noble Beasley led the organization in its efforts to reform voting rights and segregationist practices in the city. Mr. Beasley was arrested on murder charges. The *Encyclopedia of Alabama* details how the murder charges were later dropped. Those charges were proven unfounded, but he was later convicted of drug charges that many supporters claim were also manufactured. He was sentenced to life-in-prison in1990 on charges of conspiring to distribute a large amount of crack cocaine. He was released from prison in 2012 after serving nearly 23 years and died in 2014. Frederick D. Richardson became the president of NOW in 1973 after another earlier arrest of Mr. Beasley. With the urging of Ms. Dora Franklin-Finley and others, I became actively involved in civil rights activities. I started making speeches and doing work for the Mobile NAACP, working closely with Dr. Robert Gilliard, who was a board member and a dentist in Mobile.

CHAPTER 13

From Protest to Progress

BSU President's Mission to Open Doors at the University of South Alabama

Besides having a bullet almost kill me in his home, Jack Jackson was a decent stepfather. He helped me to earn money for my college education, which was a crucial part of my life. Mr. Jackson did construction, odd jobs and handiwork for a well-to-do white man named Robert N. Campbell. My stepfather sometimes took me to work with him. Mr. Campbell liked me, and engaged me in several meaningful conversations. I'm sure that he saw me as an independent worker who didn't need anyone to stand over me to get the job done. Mr. Campbell would ask me "What do you want to do with your future?" I told him that I was attending S.D. Bishop State and wanted to continue my education and become a lawyer, even though I knew it would take me another seven years. After a few of those talks with the boss, he knew that I wanted to go further in college. One day, before the job ended, Mr. Campbell came back to the worksite and asked that if he would help me accomplish my goals would I help someone else along the way. I was astounded, amazed and confused that this white man was willing to reach out and lift me up. You see, right then and there I had to change my opinions about white people. I had already found it very easy to dislike all white folks because, in my mind and the very deep places in my heart, I felt that they had brought so much hardship to Blacks. Instead of hardships, here was someone who was definitely able and willing to open up tremendous opportunities for me. He had seen and heard me and accepted my goals as a part of his own purpose in life, both spiritually and financially. He became my staunch supporter for several years. I was motivated enough to get serious about college, while rededicating my life to helping others. Not only was Mr. Campbell very supportive of me by paying tuition and buying books, he also introduced me to his family and his business ventures. I would have many opportunities to hop on private planes and travel with him and a business partner to the Carolina's. He opened his home to me so that I could live there and help his wife with jobs around their Edenton, North Carolina home. Eventually, I would end up in a home in the neighborhood when tongues began to wag about my being in the same home as his wife. Along with the business-partner-hopeful, Malcolm McLean, we would fly over thousands of acres of land while scouting out a site for a food production business. The plan was for McLean Trucking Company to move food products and for me to be a part of the legal arm of that company that would support a chain of food stores across the country. With all of these awesome plans, I didn't have to repay Mr. Campbell. He only expected me to "help someone else". Things did not work out exactly as planned, but through the years and to this present day I've done my very best to honor Mr. Campbell and his request.

At the University of South Alabama (USA), I majored in History and Political Science, with minors in Communications and African-American Studies. I earned money working for Mr. Campbell to help cover my expenses and was awarded a scholarship as a USA debater. I received both my bachelor's degrees and a master's degree in Counselor Education from the USA.

From 1972 to 1977, I gained a complete and well-rounded

education. My time there helped shape my academic and personal growth, laying the foundation for my future. As a student of color, my presence and involvement helped affirm the university as a place where members of the Black community in Mobile could thrive and achieve.

During the integration era, many white families refused to send their children to Black schools. In contrast, Black families were more willing to send their children to formerly all-white institutions, including the University of South Alabama. As the Mobile Desegregation Plan unfolded, Black schools were gradually shut down. Central High School, where I studied, had fallen into disrepair—its condition reflected a system being dismantled. I graduated with the Class of 1970, the final class before the school was closed for good. After graduation, my friend Louis Orange and I parted ways. I chose to attend Bishop State Junior College and major in Pre-Law. Louis joined the Marine Corps. Over the years, he came home between tours, and we reconnected at reunions and visits.

With few options available after Central's closure, Bishop State became a stepping stone for me. While there, I was encouraged by a group of Vietnam veterans—newly returned and still adjusting to civilian life—to run for President of the student body. Their support was humbling. My opponent, Dennis Alexander from Prichard, Alabama, was a veteran himself—older, more experienced, and respected. On election day, some veterans who supported me believed Dennis crossed a line by helping a student use the ballot machine. It led to a heated confrontation. Personally, I didn't think Dennis meant any harm. I lost the election, and it was disappointing—but it taught me an early and valuable lesson: not every good effort ends in a win.

That moment helped shape my understanding of leadership and resilience. I would later come into my own at the University of South Alabama, where I found more opportunities to lead and serve. With the steady encouragement of Robert Campbell, I discovered my purpose: to uplift others and grow into the leader I was always meant to become.

Other life-changing events also took place during my college years at Bishop State. Most significantly, I became a father. During that time, I welcomed two beautiful children into my life: my son, Alvin Taymar Williams Lovett, and my daughter, Brandie Singleton.

Becoming a father while still finding my own path was a profound shift. It made me more aware of the weight of my choices and the kind of future I wanted to build. I won't share their personal stories here — those are theirs to tell, in their own time and space. But what I will say is this: I love them with all my heart, and more. They have always been, and will always be, a source of strength and pride in my life.

After two years at Bishop State, my focus turned even more toward my education. I was determined to become a strong student. Robert Campbell — a true mentor and hero in my life — believed in me deeply. His encouragement changed my attitude and lifted my altitude. With his support, I was accepted to the University of South Alabama in Mobile.

Attending a predominantly white institution was a cultural adjustment. Up to that point, nearly all of my educational experiences had been in Black schools. It was a shift — one that came with both challenges and new growth.

Meanwhile, my close friend John Tate went on to Jackson State University in Mississippi, where he became one of the top linebackers in the nation. He played alongside three football legends: Hall-of-Famer Walter Payton, Mobile's own Robert Brazile Jr., and Don Reese. When John came home to visit, I always made sure he had a good time. In his second year, I drove to Jackson to see him play. He didn't know I was coming, and when he spotted me in the stands, he put on a show. His team won that day, and I joked that he played so well just because he saw me cheering for him.

John went on to play professional football, and even after I moved to California, I never returned to Mobile without reconnecting with him. Our bond — forged in childhood and strengthened through years of shared experiences — remained one of the most meaningful friendships of my life.

College challenged me in unexpected ways, but it also offered powerful opportunities for growth. Attending the University of South Alabama placed me at the heart of a pivotal moment in Alabama's educational history. As a Black student at a predominantly white institution, I was navigating more than just academics — I was stepping into a space that had only recently begun to open its doors to people who looked like me.

My time at USA came just after a wave of court-ordered desegregation swept through Alabama. The legacy of that shift was still fresh, and its impact was visible — in the classrooms, in the culture, and in the cautious interactions between students. That history wasn't just something I read about; I lived it, and it shaped the way I moved through campus and saw my place in the world.

Throughout history, courageous individuals and landmark events have disrupted the status quo and directly challenged the racist foundations of American education. These moments didn't just stir controversy — they reshaped the course of history.

The following cases were not just distant headlines; they shaped the educational landscape I entered as a young Black man in Alabama. They laid the groundwork for my experiences at the University of South Alabama and influenced the opportunities and obstacles I faced along the way.

Such was the case with a series of Supreme Court cases where everyday individuals challenged the segregated educational systems and started monumental changes across the country. The State of Alabama and its largest city, Mobile, were no exceptions.

One of those history-changing events involved Ms. Vivian Juanita Malone Jones. Vivian Malone attended Central High School, where she was a member of the National Honor Society and graduated in 1960. Vivian Malone was one of the first two black students to enroll at the University of Alabama in Tuscaloosa in 1963, and in 1965 became the university's first black graduate. She was made famous when George C. Wallace, the Governor of Alabama, attempted to block her and James Hood from enrolling at the all-white university.

Her parents both worked at Brookley Air Force Base; her father served in maintenance and her mother worked as a domestic servant. They emphasized the importance of receiving an education and often participated in local civil rights meetings and activities in the community. Vivian enrolled in Alabama Agricultural and Mechanical University (Alabama A & M), attended for two years and received a bachelor's degree in business education. In order to fulfill her goal of a degree in accounting, Vivian would have to transfer to another university which, unlike Alabama A & M, was fully accredited by the Southern Association of Colleges and Schools. In 1961 the local Non-Partisan Voters League had organized a plan to desegregate the University of Alabama's branch school in Mobile. It has been said that at least 200 black students had applied to the university only to have their applications rejected. The university is said to have denied admission to the applicants on the grounds of over-enrollment and closed enrollment, because of their 'quotas' already being filled or the academic performance of the students not meeting required standards. The word in the community was that the university would not admit the black students because of resistance to school desegregation. A lot of people knew that the black students who had applied to the university's branch campus in Mobile were investigated by the university's department of Public Safety, including Malone. The findings of those investigations were that all efforts to integrate the school had instigated violent retaliation from the local white community and there would be no way that much protection could be provided to Black applicants. They insisted that this situation would pose a threat to the safety of Vivian and any other students. This revelation did not deter Malone from continuing to support integration in the university and she persisted in applying to the University of Alabama to earn a degree in accounting. It would take two years of efforts by the NAACP Legal Defense and Educational Fund of Alabama, as well as, court proceedings and deliberations before Vivian Malone and James Hood were granted permission to enroll in the university by order of District Court Judge District Court, Judge Harlan Grooms in 1963. The district court had ruled that the University of Alabama's practice of denying black student admission into their university was a violation of the U. S. Supreme Court's ruling in the *Brown v. Board of Education* case. Judge Grooms had also forbidden Governor Wallace from interfering with the students' registration. On June 11, 1963, Malone and Hood, accompanied by United States Deputy Attorney General Nicholas Katzenbach and a three-car motorcade full of federal marshals, arrived at the University of Alabama's campus with the intention to enroll. Waiting for them on campus and blocking the entryway to Foster Auditorium was Governor Wallace, flanked by a group of state troopers. It's said and it appears that Wallace intended to keep true to his promise of upholding segregation in the state and stopping "integration at the schoolhouse door". It would take Katzenbach calling upon the assistance of then President John F. Kennedy to force Wallace to permit the black students' entry into the university. President Kennedy federalized the Alabama National Guard later the same day, which put them under the command of the president, rather than the governor of Alabama. One hundred guardsmen escorted Malone and Hood from their dorms back to the auditorium, where Wallace moved aside at the request of General Henry V. Graham. Malone and Hood then entered the building, albeit through another door. As she and Hood entered the building, they were surprised to be met with applause from white supporters of integration. They then entered the gym and registered as students of the university. Reports are that Malone's time spent at the University of Alabama was relatively free of conflict and threats to her safety, with the exception of a spree of bombings that occurred in November 1963 by rioting whites who were possibly angry with the integration policy. After much deliberation between the U.S. Marshal and Katzenbach, it was decided that Malone would not be taken out of school or disenrolled because of the bombings. Two years later, in 1965, Vivian Malone received a Bachelor of Arts in Business Management and became the first black student to graduate from the University of Alabama. In 2000, Vivian Malone Jones gave the commencement address at the University of Alabama, and the university bestowed on her a doctorate of humane letters. In 2004, the Alabama State Legislature honored her by passing a resolution in commemoration of her outstanding achievements. In 2017, a historical marker was installed at the Mobile County Health Department in honor of Jones. It was placed at the location of her childhood home, which is now the parking lot for the Keeler Memorial Building on the Mobile County Health Department's campus. In 2018, a street in downtown Mobile was named in her honor.

The process of desegregating the public schools in Alabama would prove to be just as difficult as it was for four-year institutions of learning. Glancing back thru history, in 1954 the well-known Brown v. the Board of Education of Topeka Kansas case ruled that the act of educating black children in schools intentionally separated from white students was unconstitutional. Suddenly school systems were charged with the responsibility of devising and implementing desegregation plans in the schools. To say that school desegregation did not proceed 'with all deliberate speed' is a mega-understatement. School desegregation was ordered by a judge in several Alabama school districts for the first week of school in September 1963, a full nine years after Brown v. Board of

Education. Desegregation of Alabama's public schools occurred in fits and starts and included several catalyzing events.

In January 1963, African American parents of students in Macon County, Alabama, had sued the Macon County Board of Education to desegregate the county's public schools. In August 1963, a federal court ordered the school board to begin integration immediately. The school board selected 13 African American students to integrate Tuskegee High School that fall. Macon County's Tuskegee High School would be the first Alabama school district to integrate. On September 2, 1963 which was scheduled to be the first day of school, then Gov. George Wallace ordered Tuskegee High closed due to "safety concerns." When Black students arrived a week later, it is reported that every White student withdrew. The brand-new private school, Macon Academy, was formed and became the first among many "desegregation academies" established in response to court-ordered desegregation of our public schools. To ensure the success of this effort at derailing desegregation, Gov. Wallace and Macon County School Board members approved the use of state funds that gave scholarships to white students who had abandoned the public school system and its Black students. The school board would later order the closure of Tuskegee High due to low enrollment. The Black students were split between all-white schools in two neighboring towns where the white students would protest for a few says and then abandon ship. Those white students would eventually transfer to Macon Academy which is now known as Macon East Academy, in Cecil, Alabama near Montgomery, Alabama.

In September of 1963, things were happening in the public

schools in Mobile County. There are newspaper accounts of Alabama State Troopers preventing Henry Hobdy (17) and Dorothy Davis (16) from entering Murphy High School in Mobile, Alabama, on Sept. 9, 1963. If you do your research, you will find an Associated Press (AP) Photo by Fred Noel on that day, showing young Hobdy reading his copy of an executive order from Gov. George Wallace stopping the pair from attending classes. After that, a federal judge would bar Wallace from any further interference with that school and Birdie Mae Davis would sue the school system in order to attend Murphy High School. On September 10, 1963, Birdie Mae Davis, Dorothy Davis and Henry Hobdy successfully desegregated Mobile schools, with the help of longtime NAACP leader in Mobile, AL., John L. LeFlore.

1970 would see a continuation of the struggle to desegregate schools at all levels in Alabama. According to Encyclopedia Britannica, the Davis v. Board of School Commissioners of Mobile County case was argued in October of 1970 but a decision was not made until April of 1971. The Court looked at the Mobile School Desegregation Plan and found it to be inadequate for desegregating schools and communities that were geographically separated and isolated, East from West by the main highway. The Mobile Plan, implemented in 1970, involved the closure of several schools at all levels. Unfortunately, my alma mater, Central High School, was on the chopping block. This made my class, the Class of '70, the last graduating class. As much as our society looks at "firsts", those "lasts" are just as impactful, if not more so.

In 1971, the US Supreme Court ruled that Mobile County's desegregation plan did not make use of all possible remedies. The lower district courts were charged with developing a more realistic plan. These so-called realistic plans involved several possibilities - restructuring attendance zones, adjusting grade structures, split-zoning and busing children out of their neighborhoods. From elementary to high schools, the reality of desegregation in my community was messy.

Unfortunately, that messiness has continued up to current times. Years after I would graduate from the University of South Alabama on April 21, 2021 Kansas Professors Bryan Mann and Annah Rogers would publish a study in the Wiley Online Library entitled "Segregation Now, Segregation Tomorrow, Segregation Forever? Racial and Economic Isolation and Dissimilarity in Rural Black Belt Schools in Alabama". They concluded that Alabama's public schools in the Black Belt, with few exceptions, were slightly more segregated than they were in 1990. This finding prompted Mann and Rogers to question whether Gov. George Wallace's 1963 infamous promise of "segregation now, segregation tomorrow, segregation forever" was ultimately kept.

While I was at the University of South Alabama, I was asked to run for president of the Black Student Union. I wasn't interested, but I was drafted and elected. That was a turning point in my life. I give credit to the motivation I received from Robert Campbell. He paid my tuition, and I am forever grateful. As President of the Black Student Union at the University of South Alabama, it took time to understand how significant my position was. I wasn't excited about being a part of the organization. My motivation was to succeed in academics, so I initially thought the responsibility would be a distraction to my goals.

The Black Student Union, before I became President, had been an organization who fought the administration, promoted protection against anti-integration, and petitioned to have the right to bear arms while going to class. Under my leadership in 1972 and 1973, there was a turning point. We had the first African-Americans on the baseball team, and the first African-Americans, since 1965, on the basketball team. One of those pioneers was Benjamin Harris, who was on the basketball team in 1967 and 1968. As President of the Black Student Union, I was able to create opportunities for us to have fundraisers. Our goal was to participate in activities relevant to our experience as African-American students. The organization was relatively new. The Black Student Union had worked as an outside group that was not accepted by the Administration. My intention, as a leader, was to bring the African American students to the mainstream. To accomplish my goals, I would meet and enjoy the support of many individuals that you will learn about in the following pages. It is unsung, untold, not written or recognized that the most significant Black Student Union chain of events to follow at the University of South Alabama was also the most impactful success story that helped explode it to its community, state and national growth of today. In the early 1970's the students and I changed the University of South Alabama to an option for success which included African Americans as an included population under its umbrella.

Janice White (Burton) studied Psychology and Education at the University of South Alabama. She was a member of the Black Student Union, who saw and accepted me as a leader, an organizer, and a humanitarian. I remember a time early on when I organized a sit-in at the university because they wouldn't give us a place to meet on campus. It seemed like they were against the black students being together. I rallied all of the "little chicken people," as Janice called them, and got them to join me. They were all scared, but I was their leader, and we did the sit-in together at the University President's office. The result was that we got our own Black Student Union office, but the space that they gave to us was an old coat check closet. If they looked for the worst place on campus, that's what they found. They gave us that closet, maybe hoping it would break us, and we didn't give them the satisfaction. Instead of being disappointed, we made the space ours and turned it into something fabulous. I liked getting people involved and keeping them motivated. Janice was motivated after that, experiencing things that she never had before. We held fundraisers for various community programs, and we walked through the neighborhoods, registering people to vote. Because Janice was a talented artist, I convinced her to paint a mural on the wall of the Black Student Union. It was a mural of Africa, from back in ancient times, to the time of modern Africa. At the end of the mural was the image of a powerful, black man wearing a big, perfect Afro, his black fist raised high in the air. You know those white folks were not ready to see that! As soon as you came up the stairs to the Black Student Union, the first thing you saw was this huge painting. You couldn't have missed it if you wanted to. A strong, African king with his big fist lifted to the sky. I wanted something that expressed who we were, so there would be no doubt that it was the Black Student Union. It was our world, and I wasn't afraid of any consequences. I completely supported Janice, every step of the way. Janice's talent was unmistakable, even though it sometimes looked as though the university was getting her down. She came from a conservative family and had attended Catholic school. I helped her to get out of her shell and got her active in the Black Student Union. It worked! Janice put her heart and soul into that mural and made a grand statement. Everybody who came up those stairs came face to face with Black Power! There was a 17-year period when Janice and I didn't see each other. However, we re-connected on Facebook and she stayed in touch with me all this time. A good friend to this day, Janice recently shared memories of her time at the University of South Alabama. She found her power through her artistic talents and felt that I had helped somehow. Janice told me that I maintained a spirit to help make people more important than I was. Of course, I appreciate the praise, but it was never about me. It was always about helping the neighborhood, helping people get homes, helping people get food, helping people get their lights on, and making sure everybody was taken care of in terms of their health. I'm happy that Janice took away that impression of me as a person. My goal was about bringing change for the betterment of mankind. Folks believed in me. I was using my voice, and people listened. She said I was a mover and a shaker. I didn't like putting attention on myself. Janice recognized my humility then. And I'm still humble now.

Every step in my life was a step that the Lord took with me. All steps which had to be taken, given the sacrifices and struggles of so many before me who, in making a way for themselves prepared the way for me.

My time with the Black Student Union at the University of South Alabama provided many opportunities for me, both academically and otherwise. Moncenya Smith was a gorgeous woman who became an active member of the

Black Student Union. One of the first things I noticed was her big Angela Davis afro. She was light-skinned, with a very shapely body, a beautiful smile, and a sparkling personality. An avid supporter of mine, she became very involved with everything I did, and there was an attraction between us. I was hesitant to start anything with her because I already had two children. However, Moncenya was determined to make me her man. I spent a lot of time fighting against the relationship, but she won that fight and I was happy about it. We began dating and became inseparable, but that's another story.

Our Student Union became actively involved in the issues of the day. In 1973, one of the first important issues to come up was a decision by the Alabama State Legislature, which allowed African Americans to participate in the political arena for the first time. There had never been more opportunities for black people, not since Reconstruction in 1865. Black people had made progress in several sectors. They became involved in politics and created change. Our people were finally able to go to Woolworth's or S & H Kress and order a hot dog or hamburger without having to go to the back door. It was inspiring. I began to feel a calling! I thought that it was the perfect time for me to be of service to a great cause. I wanted to be one of the people involved in positive change. So, with me leading about 300 African-American students at that time, we took to the streets of Mobile generating voter interest and encouraging voter registration.

Our connections to the political arena in our community came through Tina Allen, who was known to many as a great artist. Tina Allen was known for her sculpted monuments of prominent African Americans. She had earned a bachelor of fine arts degree from the University of South Alabama in 1978 and had hosted a local television show for nearly ten years. People have described her art as a history in bronze because she always focused on important black historical figures and wanted to portray them through sculpture. She also had periods of her work focused specifically on black men and then she turned her interest to black women. There is a display of her work at the Charles R. Drew University of Medicine and Science in Los Angeles. Tina was a campaign manager who had been on a television show at Mobile's WALA-TV 10, an NBC affiliate. She was one of the people who opened the door for me to be on television some years later. While I was at the university she was running the political campaign representing J. Gary Cooper, America's first black Ambassador to Jamaica. There were three African-Americans elected to office through our efforts. J. Gary Cooper was one. The others were Cain Kennedy, who was Alabama's first black circuit court judge, and John LeFlore, a Mobile civil rights leader. In a nutshell, those three men were the first African-Americans elected to the Alabama State Legislature, with the help of the Black Student Union of the University of South Alabama. I am both humbled and pleased to report that all of this happened under my leadership – a feather in the cap of Alvin Lovett.

Being involved in that political effort launched me into the limelight in a new way. I thank God that I had the opportunity. John LeFlore and another man named Joseph Langham brought people in Mobile together, and I was a part of that effort.

I also became a member of the debate team at the University of South Alabama with another black student, Ken Simon. He became a lawyer, a judge, and a good friend. Ken is also on the Board of Trustees for the University of South Alabama. A lot of African-Americans went to Alabama State University, Alabama A&M University, or out of state to an HBCU (Historically Black College or University). However, there was significant growth in African-Americans attending the University of South Alabama, and I worked tirelessly to be partially responsible for that change.

Through the Speaker's Bureau, our Black Student Union was able to invite author Alex Haley to speak. Haley shared with us how he honed his writing skills by writing love letters for his buddies during his twenty years in the U. S. Coast Guard. He had just finished writing the Autobiography of Malcolm X and was working on a personal genealogy project. Unfortunately, he ran out of money to go to Africa for his final research to trace certain words to a particular area and tribe. He had to find the meaning of the African word for guitar or fiddle, and also the word for a type of drum. So, the Black Student Union stepped up to help him out. We did many things to help. We produced a play called '*The Blacker Side of Life*' and had soul food dinners for sale to raise money for him to make that trip. When I look back on what we accomplished I have to shake my head! Alex Haley's trip to Africa was made possible with our help! He finished writing his epic novel, '*Roots: The Saga of an American Family*', one of the greatest books ever written about the black experience in this country. It was a huge success, and we had a tiny part in it. We knew that we wouldn't be known to the world, but what we accomplished was significant in allowing that project to soar. Our goal was to help all Americans to be tolerant and accepting of black people and to change the landscape of our people's lives.

Our Black Student Union invited Dr. Alvin Poussaint, currently Dean of Students at Harvard Medical School, and author of many books on the mental health of black people. His focus has been on African American children and ways to help raise them in a racially charged world. In the 1980s, Dr. Poussaint became a consultant on the Cosby Show. He shared studies about how we black people see ourselves as inferior. One study he presented was the "doll test," which was created in the 1940s by married psychologists Kenneth Bancroft Clark and Mamie Phipps Clark, based on her Howard University master's thesis. It was designed to study how segregation affects black children. I know that it affected my life. It influenced how I see myself as somebody to be proud of, and helped shape my views of myself and my people.

Nikki Giovanni, the famed poet, writer, and activist, came to our school to speak. She said that we don't have to stay in the same place where we grew up. In a few hours, you could be on a plane somewhere, in another country. I would have never chosen to leave Mobile to create a new life in California if Nikki Giovanni had not inspired me to travel, and see a world outside of everything I had ever known.

I imagine it is impressive that I was able to bring people like Alex Haley, Dr. Alvin Poussaint, and Nikki Giovanni to a predominantly white college campus. I even brought Jessie Jackson to Mobile, so I did well. It was a blessing that I was able to get those things done. Even high-powered people, in high powered positions, sometimes don't get things done the way our small army of energized Black students did at the University of South Alabama.

Having such powerful and influential people in my life never over-shadowed the impact of my friends throughout my life. One of my childhood friends, Arthur Mack, also went to predominantly black Bishop State before starting his junior year at the University of South Alabama. It was as much of a culture shock for him as it was for me. I could not only imagine but know personally how challenging it was for him to come into a mostly white college. I helped him with his transition as much as I could and encouraged him to get involved with the Black Student Union. I was in my senior year and wanted Arthur to become more culturally aware, so he spent a lot of time with Moncenya and me. We were a cool couple, and he enjoyed being in our presence.

Throughout much of my time at USA, my focus continued to be towards my ambition to be a lawyer. At that time, Al Stokes was my first black instructor at the USA's Political Science Department. His father, Rev. Stokes, was my grandfather's pastor at Mt. Olive Baptist Church #1, as well as, one of my grandfather's great friends. Al Stokes, was the first black professor that I took a course from in college. I initially got a D in German History from another professor's class and thought it meant that I wasn't good enough to be a lawyer. I was an honor student before that, so my confidence got rocked. But it forced me to work harder and reminded me not to glide through life. I elevated my focus, got an A from Al Stokes, and made the Dean's List. I was very grateful to him. He pushed me academically and helped me to remember who I was and what I could accomplish.

After graduating from South Alabama, with a double degree in History and Political Science my ambition to be a lawyer was stronger than ever. I also received secondary degrees in African-American Studies and Public Speaking. I wanted to go to law school at the University of Alabama, and made a trip with George Smith, Roosevelt Simmons, and Wesley "Porky" James, for a pre-visit. While we were there, we met A. G. Gaston, who was speaking at the University of Alabama Law School. As I mentioned earlier, he was the richest black man in America at that time. Mr. Gaston was a multi millionaire, but he couldn't speak proper English. He made a special request for African-American students to attend a special seminar at the University of Alabama because he wanted students to come and work for him. We laughed at the way he spoke and were embarrassed by his incorrect grammar. But he wasn't embarrassed at all. He asked if we would rather say, "I is rich, or I am poor?" A. G. Gaston said that a coin has two flat sides and a round side that rolls out of your hand into somebody else's pocket. A new suit with a hole in the pocket is not as good as an old suit with no holes. It's not how much you make, but how much you keep that can make you rich.

George, Roosevelt, Porky, and I drove back from the University of Alabama with excitement. We were a little bad as we celebrated with bottles of wine. We sang James Brown and Jackie Wilson songs. Porky sat in the back seat. He was one of the greatest football players around, along with my buddy, John Tate. All of a sudden, Porky put down his wine and began singing *Amazing Grace*. It was a revelation as we witnessed the Lord enter his body. At that moment, Porky had received a calling to preach. His spirit was charged to carry a cross, and he eventually became a great preacher.

Wesley "Porky" James was one of my best friends and advised me on many things. Porky would go on to achieve much success as a pastor of the Franklin Street Missionary Baptist Church and an esteemed civic leader for citizens of the Mobile and Prichard, Alabama communities.

I did not get accepted at the University of Alabama School of Law. During the entrance exam, my score wasn't high enough. I was devastated about failing that test, but I was not going to give up. My challenge was in taking the tests, which were found to be culturally biased and discriminatory toward minorities. I needed help with preparing to pass the LSAT. Rutgers University had a seminar, and I was able to go there for training. I didn't know what would happen if I failed after that. Once again, I had to question my decision to be a lawyer. However, it was going to take a year after the LSAT coaching to get the results. Instead of law school, I went to the University of South Alabama's graduate program and decided to get my Master's Degree. I got a degree in counseling and became a Counselor of Education. That was something which enhanced my understanding of how people think, especially those who don't walk in my shoes or wear my skin. It was a very challenging period. I would have followed Michael Figures, who was one of the first three black students to graduate from there. He eventually served in the Alabama Senate from the 33rd District in Mobile County from 1978 until he died of an aneurysm in 1996. His widow, Senator Vivian Figures is currently serving, initially being elected to finish out her deceased husband's term of office.

CHAPTER 14

Broadcasting Revolution

The Man Behind Visions TV Show

My life went through a prosperous period. A period where I had finished college and had begun a new career. I got my investor's license at the Atlanta Investment Training Institute. There were no other blacks there. I started a job at Investors Diversified Services (IDS), one of the largest mutual funds companies in America. I was an investor and a stockbroker. People hadn't had a black stockbroker in Mobile, nor in that southern part of Alabama. Working at IDS allowed me to play a part in changing a lot of people's lives for the better. Learning how to manage money and set up household budgets allowed me to launch into a career that helped my community. I became involved in events that impacted history. When I was with IDS, I was doing well. I shared my knowledge and showed Arthur Mack how to make money and save money. Arthur said that his daughter is very frugal as a result of him passing on my advice. I am happy to know that I had a significant impact on his life, and he has been able to pass it on to the next generation. We lost track of each other around 1977 after Arthur went into the Navy.

Moncenya and I dated for four years before she graduated. We loved each other deeply and looked forward to building a life together. After her graduation, we got married and planned what we hoped would be a joyful future. She started working at a nationwide department store, and we took a honeymoon trip to Florida to celebrate the beginning of our life together.

But during that honeymoon, something happened that would test our relationship early on.

At the time, I was deeply involved in a major financial opportunity that connected me to many of my family members, friends, and associates—men who worked as longshoremen and were members of the International Longshoremen's Association. These hard working men trusted me to help improve their future. They were prepared to invest $18 million of their pension fund into Investors Diversified Services (IDS), working through me. This money represented their retirement security—the result of decades of backbreaking labor loading and unloading cargo ships at the State Docks.

Historically, those pension funds were managed by businessmen who had little connection to the laborers themselves. As a result, the longshoremen earned minimal interest, which meant meager retirement payouts. Meanwhile, the businessmen used that money for indirect loans and private ventures, enriching themselves while the men who actually earned the money were left behind. I found this unjust. Most of the labor force at that time was African-American, and I strongly believed that they deserved better—especially when double-digit interest returns were available through IDS.

Of course, this effort wasn't welcomed by the powerful elite who benefitted from the current system. I received warnings to back off and direct my attention elsewhere. No African-American before me had pushed for financial justice on behalf of the longshoremen. But I persisted. After much resistance, I was finally granted a formal meeting—an opportunity to present the IDS proposal and secure the investment that could change thousands of lives.

There was just one problem: the meeting was scheduled for the middle of my honeymoon.

I asked Moncenya to attend the meeting with me, but she refused. Understandably, she wanted us to focus on our time together. Still, I made the painful decision to leave her in Florida—less than 100 miles from Mobile—and return alone to attend the meeting.

That decision strained our marriage from the very beginning. In my mind, I believed I had no choice. I couldn't bear the thought of letting all those men down. But in reality, there are always choices—and consequences. That moment taught me that leadership often demands sacrifice, but it also revealed how easily personal relationships can be caught in the crossfire.

My mother's brother, Ballard, served in the Merchant Marines. While he was overseas, he left his furniture and many treasured items in a storage garage. Around that same time, Moncenya's family was planning a reunion, and I offered to help by lending them beds and other furnishings from that storage unit. It allowed them to accommodate out-of-town guests comfortably.

While Uncle Ballard was away, he continued receiving his allotment from the Merchant Marines. Because he couldn't read or write, he entrusted me with managing his finances. I paid his bills and kept organized records. I was also named the heir to his estate.

However, tension arose when a family member—concerned about my role—began questioning the arrangement. When Uncle Ballard returned home from sea and discovered that I had loaned out his furniture and hadn't retrieved it, that same relative asked to see the financial records I kept. I had no issue with that and shared everything openly.

But once she saw the amount of the allotment coming in, she began to stir conflict. I believe she influenced Uncle Ballard into thinking I was taking advantage of him. Later, I was told she even encouraged him to remove me from his will—despite the fact that she and her family were already financially secure.

I learned a valuable lesson during this particular trial in my life. In life, you can work hard to be of kind goodwill and fairness to your loved ones in your family or other relationships. You can dedicate your life to do the right thing for your loved ones by being honest and loyal to the best interest of any person you help. Watch out for someone wearing sheep's clothing who has a different objective. That objective may be to rob, steal and destroy you for their personal gains.

To make matters even worse, my Grandmother, Alvenia, died during that time, and Uncle Ballard got angry at me all over again. Family members came to the house after the funeral and left with several things that belonged to him. Maybe they thought they were taking souvenirs from my grandmother's estate. In any case, Uncle Ballard made me responsible for the losses. That way he felt justified in cutting me out of his will. I did not feel that I had lost anything from being disinherited because my service to him was not to gain personal material items. I just needed to show him love through offering him my talents, my gifts of service. Even then, I could sense that God had a greater gift and calling in my life to help people. Personal, material gain did not motivate me, as I learned that some people are turned on by stealing, robbing and destroying at all cost. It seemed to excite them. I found that simply being in a family will not protect you from vicious people who seek personal gain. Some of those same people will use God's words in their daily lives to take advantage of honest people.

It was 1977 when I met Douglas Wicks. He was from Mobile but lived in Los Angeles, where he went to UCLA and graduated in 1973. Then he went to Columbus, Mississippi for 2 1/2 years and moved back to Mobile in 1976, where we met the following year. He was involved in the Miss Black Alabama beauty pageant, which he sponsored for a couple of years. My wife was a volunteer for the pageant, and I helped, too. When Douglas and I first met, it was like we had known each other for a long time. He was a big, tall guy, but warm, cordial and willing to help. He got to know us very well. Douglas's sister, Lillie Tolin, and I were also very close. Douglas was a few years older than me and was involved in a lot of civic activities. I was willing to help him, as well. He had a community based-TV show where he talked about community affairs. Doug hosted the show and even had my wife host a couple of times. Eventually, I began hosting the show. Douglas didn't think that I would do a good job, but he soon changed his tune. Lillie said I was better than him, and my wife. If I wanted another profession, Douglas said that I had the personality and charisma to be just as good as Arsenio Hall. Douglas would go on to become the first African American to win a seat on the Mobile County Commission. This was the highest political ranking in Mobile County in Alabama.

In my twenties, I did what young men do and was full of hope and opportunity. The skills that I exhibited throughout my life, as a salesman, are the skills that I showed early in life. I was successful and made a lot of money selling insurance. I proved myself to be trustworthy with my gift of communication and my integrity. Those things were important to me. I never had harsh words with Douglas, because disagreements were things that I worked to diffuse. Douglas was more hyper, intense, and professionally driven. I could step in a room, say something to

Douglas, and have him smile. I always knew that Douglas was going to be a 'Big Man' in Mobile, Alabama some day and I told him so. Then, I would laugh and remind him to keep eating those Krispy Kreme doughnuts! Ha!

My radio work began with WBLX Radio FM in Mobile. Myrland Clarke, a lifelong friend from Lily Baptist Church and former president of the University of South Alabama Black Student Union, was the account executive there. He helped launch a program called *Ain't Gonna Let Nobody Turn Us Around*, which I co-hosted with my brother-in-law, Ronald (Smith) Ali. I also hosted a separate radio program on WGOK called *Sunday at One*, which allowed me to engage directly with the community on topics that mattered.

My entry into television came through *Visions*, a program originally hosted by Dr. Yvonne Kennedy—an influential leader who later became National President of Delta Sigma Theta Sorority and a member of the Alabama State Legislature. After being interviewed as a guest, I was eventually invited to take over hosting duties. I served as host of *Visions* for nearly a decade, using the platform to spark conversations and bring positive change across Alabama.

Visions was a public service television show that addressed issues affecting African Americans in the Gulf Coast viewing area. I served as the host of the show, while Floyd King was the producer. It aired on Sunday mornings and was more than just a broadcast—it was a platform for advocacy, education, and empowerment.

The show functioned as an extension of the work done by Neighborhood Organized Workers (NOW), a grassroots movement dedicated to advancing civil rights in Mobile. Later, that mission continued through the group *People United to Advance the Dream*, currently led by Reverend David Edwards. This organization is best known today for coordinating the annual Martin Luther King Jr. celebration in Mobile, Alabama.

The head anchors of the local television stations would usually interview celebrities and well-known people who came to town. However, big names began to come and talk to me first on *Visions,* instead of going to the national reporters. Lou Rawls came on the show to talk about his *Parade of Stars* for the United Negro College Fund. Willard Scott from NBC's Today Show was a guest. He was a white man who chose to come on a black show. Other prominent people allowed me to get the first interview with them when they came to town, like Coretta Scott King and Jesse Jackson. That's what threw the pebbles into the water that created the ripple to push for Martin Luther King, Jr. Holiday.

On *Visions*, we took the initiative and started putting the message out. Alabama had a set of issues that other states didn't have. There was an intensity and a danger when dealing with our racial issues. We had to fight for everything. Black people got harsher prison sentences, for example. Nothing was equal. Trash pickup in black areas was every two weeks but it was more frequent pick-ups in white areas. Black people could only get car loans for used cars, as a rule. School books for black students were second-hand. White schools got brand new books. The same thing with musical instruments, too. We challenged all of these things on the show. We kept it going to the point where others fell in line. They removed Washington's Birthday and Lincoln's Birthday to have Presidents Day and to make room for Martin Luther King Day. However, as of this writing in 2023, the State of

Alabama still celebrates Robert E. Lee's birthday on the same day as M. L. K. Day. Robert E. Lee was actually born on the 19th of January but as the commander of the Confederate Army, in both Alabama and Mississippi he got top billing. Coincidentally, the State of Alabama is also the last remaining state to continue a legal state holiday which celebrates the birth of Jefferson Davis, Confederate President. My beloved home-state still has a lot of work to do when it comes to falling in line with the rest of America on these crucial changes.

My television show 'Visions' was the vehicle for many prominent individuals and issues in our community. Jimmy Dallas relied on me for counsel and television exposure. He had an idea and wanted to get information out about a caring center for seniors that was second to none. He eventually built one of the most beautiful buildings in the area. It was called the Community Convalescent Center. This building is currently across the street from the Dearborn Street YMCA near Downtown Mobile and the old Negro Library. All of these buildings are down MLK Jr. Avenue from Lovett's Funeral Chapel. My television show 'Visions with Alvin Lovett' contributed significantly to the promotion and success of the Dearborn Street YMCA, the Negro Library, the Community Convalescent Center, the International Longshoremen's Association, the Orange Grove Public Project Developmental Programs, and so much more.

Franklin Primary Health Center is a non-profit, federally qualified health center founded in 1975 by Dr. Marilyn Aiello and a group of concerned citizens who recognized the need for quality health care in the under-served Davis Avenue community (now Dr. Martin Luther King, Jr. Avenue). Dr. James Alexander Franklin was a physician, scholar, and humanitarian who faithfully served his community for over 60 years. They named the center after him. Dr. Franklin was known to have folks with high blood pressure sent to him. Several nurses would get together on weekends to check blood pressure in the community. Sadie Horn, Rose Young, and Marshall Hunt worked in an office where they coordinated testing. Mr. Charles White understood public health. He came on the show, too. Under his leadership as CEO, Franklin Primary Health Center continues to ensure that everyone, no matter who they are or what they have, has access to quality health care services. I am thankful to have played a role in the early development of Franklin Primary Health Center in Mobile, Alabama. My role may have been overlooked or forgotten by some. That fact is what has motivated me to write 'Alabama Buttermilk' to bring awareness and set the record straight about so many names of heroes who have not been recognized.

Commonwealth National Bank was black-owned, and created by a group who sold shares which could be purchased by citizens. The group of men asked me to put information about the bank on my TV show, *Visions*, to help get the message out. I served on the community Board of Directors for Commonwealth National Bank. As part of a black bank, I helped to show people how to acquire wealth and changed their attitudes about money. Later, as a representative of Investors Diversified Services, I expanded my skills even further and was handling money for many of the churches. They transferred their funds to me. A person can't make that kind of impact without being noticed.

Investors Diversified Services (IDS) was the nation's largest mutual funds company. I was among the first African Americans in Alabama and Mobile to work with IDS in the financial services industry. What a difference I was able to make involving millions of dollars! This was both an honor and a historic role to play during that time period. Other names to be remembered as pioneers of financial services in Mobile thru IDS are Ronald (Smith) Ali, Lillie Wicks-Tolin, Leon Smith, Tina Allen, Jane Baker-Nettles, William H. Franklin, Sr. and Betty Davis. It is my honor to include this *IDS Roll Call* in 'Alabama Buttermilk'. Mobile should recognize Henry Davenport, Sr. for his financial contribution to the people of South Alabama.

CHAPTER 15

The Last Lynching

Michael Donald, Herndon Avenue, and the Death of the Klan

One of my aunts in Mobile had a caretaker who I will refer to as Miss C. We initially met by phone because my aunt was always talking about me, and Miss C was curious about who I was. One day I called from Compton to speak with Miss C, and she said that God had put us together. On March 21, 1981, she was a witness to something that forever changed her life and the lives of everyone in Mobile. After more than 38 years she still doesn't want to reveal herself, but she remembers it like it was yesterday.

On that fateful morning, when Miss C came out of her front door, on Herndon Avenue on her way to work, she saw her friend, who lived next door, sitting in her car with her hands up to her head, unable to speak. Miss C ran to get the woman's husband to see what was wrong with her friend. When her neighbor came out to check on his wife, they both saw the woman pointing to the sky. She looked up and then looked again. Lord have mercy! She saw a young man hanging from a tree, and it shook her. Never in a million years would she expect to see something like that. The memory is still crystal clear. The young man's name was Michael Donald, and he was only 19 years old. There was nothing Miss C could do because she was in shock. She had a son of her own, and the thought of him being vulnerable made her sick. Michael was hanging from a tree a few houses down. She remembers seeing a lot of blood as daylight was breaking. Other neighbors called the cops. She was so scared at that point. By listening to the news, and how people talked, the murderers were Klansmen who stayed on Herndon Avenue. They lived on the other side of the street, directly across from where they found Michael. No one ever asked her anything about the incident. She just saw the boy hanging there. It made her sick for days.

Eventually, different stories began coming out in the news. The day Michael died, he was walking to get cigarettes for his sister. The Klan rolled up on him, asking if he knew where some street was. Then they forced him into the car, carried him over the bay, beat him up really bad, and then cut his throat. That's why he had so much blood on his shirt. They also cut off his penis, as they often did during historical lynchings. Further details of his murder were even more horrific. The Klansmen were saying that some black man got away with killing a police officer in Birmingham, AL. Police initially claimed that Michael's death was the result of a drug deal that went wrong, but his mother insisted that was not the truth. Beulah Mae Donald knew her son was better than that.

It is a fact that some stories never come out in the news. This is the case with a story that was told to me by a trusted family member. One of my cousins gave me an account of what almost happened on that fateful day when the Klan was looking for a victim – someone to kill in place of the black man who allegedly 'got away' with killing the police officer. The story goes that three white men were in a car traveling on Davis Avenue. Her father was walking to a phone booth. He needed to call his wife to come and pick him up so he could get home. It was late, almost midnight. The car pulled up to him, at which time, the older man in the back seat sat up, leaning forward. He looked at her dad and told the others "We don't want no old nigger". With that being said, they drove off. Her dad saw the car go up two blocks heading towards Broad Street but turning on Kennedy Street. That is where they found a young man – Michael Donald. This happened on a Saturday, the 21st of March, in 1981. In the days that followed, Mobile would be rocked and assaulted by stories of a young black man's body found hanging in a tree on Herndon Ave. The investigation of this horrific murder would stall for over a year, until U.S. Senator and attorney for the Donald case, Michael Figures, got the local FBI involved and a new inquiry was launched. That inquiry resulted in the arrest, trials and convictions of local Ku Klux Klan members James Knowles and Henry Francis Hays. Hays was sentenced to the death penalty. Knowles was sentenced to life imprisonment.

The wheels of justice tend to grind pretty slowly sometimes. As it happened, my cousin said that in 1996 she saw news accounts of Hays' upcoming date with destiny – his execution date. She ran to her father and asked if the man on the television was the same one who passed over him, because he was "too old". Her dad said "Yes" and he was sure of it! In the early morning hours of June 6, 1997, at 12:18am, Henry Francis Hays was executed after being convicted of what was described as the "lynching-style death" of 19-year-old Michael Donald. 42-year-old Hays' execution would happen in the Alabama electric chair 'Yellow Mama'. It would be the first time in over half a century that a white would be executed for killing a black. It would, however, not be the first (or last) time that the Lovett family would come so very close and brush up against history in the making.

It was a tragic loss and could have been any black person's child. Any brother, father, grandfather or cousin. That was a sad day in the life of Miss C. They cut down the tree that they took Michael Donald's body from and said that they would never allow it to regrow. Since then, she has moved, but continues to drive through the area. The news announced that the city would never let that tree grow back. Yet, it's the biggest tree around.

The prosecution of Michael Donald's murderers in both criminal and civil trials resulted in murder convictions and sentences. Henry Francis Hays was the son of Bennie Jack Hays, the second highest-ranking official in the Alabama Klan. Henry Hays was arrested in 1983, tried and sentenced to death. He was executed in 1997. It was the first execution carried out in Alabama since 1913, for a white-on-black crime. James Knowles, the younger man, was sentenced to life in prison after pleading guilty and testifying against his partner. Henry Hays was the only known KKK member to be executed in the 20th century for the murder of an African-American. A third defendant, Benjamin Franklin Cox, Jr. was convicted of being an accomplice and sentenced to life in prison. They charged the elder Hays as an accomplice for allegedly ordering the lynching. The first trial ended in a mistrial, and he died before a second trial started.

Senator Michael Figures, who also was an attorney and civil rights leader, was one of the founders of the Alabama New South Coalition. He represented Mrs. Donald, who filed a civil suit during that time against the local KKK and the United Klans of America (U. K. of A.) to which the attackers belonged. She also accomplished it with the help of Morris Dees, co-founder of the Southern Poverty Law Center. In 1987, the all-white jury found the United Klans of America guilty and awarded Mrs. Donald damages of $7 million, which bankrupted the organization. The case against the KKK set a precedent in the United States for legal action against other racist groups.

Before Michael Donald's mother died in 1988, she broke the Klan. They couldn't afford to pay her the money that was awarded to her by the court. They gave her the deed to the United Klans headquarters in Tuscaloosa, Alabama. It was valued at $225,000. Mrs. Donald sold the headquarters for over

$50,000. She moved from the projects and into her own home with the money she got from the sale of the KKK headquarters. Mrs. Donald died a year later. The killing of Michael divided the City of Columbus. I continued to shine a light on that story. Jeff Sessions, who later became the Attorney General in President Donald Trump's administration, was involved in that area of the judicial system at that time. "The powers that be" felt the need to protect the KKK. I felt the need to expose them for killing Michael. Years later, in 2006, the City of Mobile renamed Herndon Avenue to Michael Donald Avenue.

CHAPTER 16

Hitting Rock Bottom

The First Cut Wasn't the Knife

After seven years of marriage, Moncenya and I began to experience growing conflict. Our lives had slowly drifted in different directions. I was gaining more visibility through television and becoming increasingly involved in community work. She was committed to her career with the Urban League and remained active in Alpha Kappa Alpha Sorority. While we still shared a home, we were often living separate lives.

Our Sundays revealed just how different our routines had become. Moncenya, who was Catholic, would attend early morning mass and then join me at my church, Truevine. After service, she would head home while I continued making rounds—visiting friends, checking on relatives, and offering support to grieving families at local funeral homes. I also made time to connect with clients and their families, many of whom relied on me not just professionally but personally. Somewhere along the way, I began stopping by nightclubs, more for social connection than entertainment. But even those brief stops added to the distance growing between us.

All of that activity didn't leave much time or presence for my marriage. I wasn't an elected official, but I was always in the community—supporting causes, showing up for others, building relationships. In a way, I was campaigning without a campaign. But in doing so, I lost sight of the one relationship that should have received more of my attention.

When Moncenya told me she wanted a divorce, I was blindsided. I didn't see it coming, and the heartbreak left me confused and unsure of what had gone wrong. Looking back, I realize I had a narrow understanding of what it meant to be a good husband. I believed that because I was never physically or verbally abusive—and because I tried to be respectful and present—I was doing enough. In my mind, that made me better than many men I had seen growing up.

But marriage requires more than simply avoiding harm. It demands presence, partnership, and emotional connection—things I often gave to others in the community before offering them at home. I thought attending church, serving others, and staying out of obvious trouble made me a decent man. And while those things mattered, they weren't a substitute for real intimacy, communication, and prioritizing my marriage. I learned too late that doing what you think is "enough" doesn't always meet the needs of the one you love.

In the midst of processing my divorce, life didn't slow down. Just as I was trying to make sense of the emotional chaos at home, another crisis pulled me in a completely different direction. My mother's brother, Ballard Williams, a Merchant Marine, had fallen ill while aboard a ship and was taken to Clark Air Force Base in the Philippines. Knowing how particular he was about his health, my mother asked me to fly there and check on him personally.

When I arrived in Manila, I was disoriented and exhausted. I caught a small open-air taxi cart from the airport, with all my luggage exposed in the back. At one point, the driver abruptly stopped to use a restroom and left me sitting alone on the side of the road for several minutes—vulnerable, uncertain, and carrying more than just physical baggage. That moment, though brief, captured exactly how I felt at the time: exposed, unsettled, and far from anything familiar.

Manila was a city full of contrast—rich with culture but shadowed by visible poverty and desperation. I saw children struggling to survive in heartbreaking conditions. Many young girls were exploited and pushed into brothels, while groups of boys, seemingly abandoned, roamed the streets in search of food or opportunity. One afternoon, as I sat vulnerable in an open taxi cart, a group of those boys surrounded me. In an instant, I was stabbed and robbed of my belongings. I was left bleeding and disoriented, alone in a foreign country with nothing but the clothes on my back.

By what I can only describe as divine intervention, I crossed paths with a kind Filipino woman who offered to help me get to Clark Air Force Base. I stayed with her for a day as I recovered. Despite having very little herself, she found a way to gather money to support my journey—hoping that, in time, I could return the favor. Her generosity reminded me that even in the darkest moments, compassion can still reach you.

When I finally arrived at Clark Air Force Base, I was met with grim news. The doctors told me that Uncle Ballard had exhibited severe flu-like symptoms, but they admitted they had never seen anything quite like it. Despite their efforts, he had not responded to treatment and had passed away shortly before I arrived. I was devastated. After traveling halfway around the world to bring him home, I was told that, for reasons never fully explained, his remains could not be sent back to the United States.

Instead, I was handed a small bundle of his belongings—tokens of a life that deserved a far better farewell. I boarded a plane alone, carrying his memory but not his body. At the time, I was filled with confusion and sorrow. In the years since, I've come to believe that Uncle Ballard's death was an early case of what we would later come to know as AIDS. It was a new and terrifying illness, misunderstood by the medical community and shrouded in silence and stigma. His death marked not only a personal loss, but also a glimpse into a public health crisis that would claim millions in the years to follow.

CHAPTER 17

Public Victory, Private Defeat

When the Applause Fades and the Mirror Breaks

In time, someone entered my life who would change its direction in ways I never expected. Dr. Maria Moman Peterson was a gifted physician, specializing in Gynecology and Obstetrics. She graduated from Fisk University and went on to earn her medical degree from Howard University.

What set Maria apart wasn't just her credentials—it was her heart. She had a generous spirit and an unwavering commitment to serve. While other doctors restricted Medicaid patients to one day a week, Maria welcomed everyone, every day. Her patients included those with private insurance, those paying cash, and many who relied on Medicaid. Often, she treated people knowing she would lose money—but she believed care shouldn't depend on income. Her compassion left a lasting impression on me and on the countless lives she touched.

One day, while hanging a mirror in Maria's apartment, it slipped from my hands and sliced open my forearm. At that point, we hadn't known each other long, and she was hesitant to treat the wound herself. She didn't want me to associate the injury—or any pain—with her. Instead, she called a colleague, another physician, and sent me to his office to get stitches. I appreciated her concern, but I didn't realize the day was far from over.

After leaving the doctor's office, I went to my insurance office to pick up the day's deposits I needed to deliver to the bank. While driving down Airport Boulevard near I-65 in Mobile, another car struck mine. The impact was violent, and I suffered severe head and facial injuries. Inside the car, money and blood were scattered everywhere—a chaotic, surreal scene. I was hospitalized for an extended period. My District Manager stepped in, retrieved the money, and handled the situation with care and professionalism. It was another near-death experience—one that left both physical and emotional scars, and a deeper appreciation for life's fragility.

Even though we were no longer married, Moncenya came to the hospital to check on me after the accident. I appreciated her concern during such a difficult time. By then, Maria had stepped in to oversee my medical care, not only as a doctor but as someone who was becoming an important part of my life. She made it clear to the hospital staff that she would be managing my treatment and that everything related to my recovery would go through her.

My face had been badly disfigured in the crash—severe trauma that required extensive reconstruction. Maria took it upon herself to find a highly skilled plastic surgeon, one known across the country for his work. Thanks to her persistence and support, the surgeon was able to restore my face well enough that I could eventually return to television. Her care during that time went far beyond medicine—it was personal, steady, and deeply committed.

Maria and I shared a wedding day that felt larger than life—one of the biggest celebrations Mobile had seen in years. The ceremony was held at Truevine Missionary Baptist Church, and the entire wedding party arrived in antique cars, adding a timeless elegance to the occasion. Our reception in the Daughters of the American Revolution building in DeTonti Square had the feel of a concert, with some of the region's most beloved gospel singers lifting the room in celebration.

For me, it was more than just a public event—it was a deeply personal turning point. After everything I had been through, standing at the altar with Maria felt like a moment of redemption and grace. The city buzzed with headlines about a local businessman marrying a prominent physician, but beyond the spotlight, I felt humbled and hopeful. I was starting a new chapter—not just with a remarkable woman, but with a renewed sense of purpose, surrounded by faith, music, and love.

After I married Maria and became a stepfather to her three children, it was my first time having full-time parenting responsibilities within a marriage. Although they were not biologically mine, I considered them my own. I wanted to be a strong, present father—but the transition was harder than I expected. I began to question whether I was living up to the role. The demands of parenting sometimes collided with my professional responsibilities. There were mornings when I'd be on my way to open my insurance office by 8 a.m., only to get a call: "Dad, I forgot my homework." I'd turn around, rush back home, and drop off whatever they needed—arriving late to open the office, flustered and behind schedule.

In the world of business, punctuality is often perceived as a reflection of professionalism. I felt that being late cast me in a negative light—not just as a businessman, but as a Black businessman already working against long-standing stereotypes. Those moments forced me to learn how to balance fatherhood with career expectations. I was navigating two roles that rarely paused long enough for me to catch my breath.

At the same time, I was entrusted with major responsibilities at Truevine Missionary Baptist Church. I served on the Trustee Board and chaired the church's building committee. We were planning the construction of a new sanctuary on Stone Street and Davis Avenue (now Martin Luther King Jr. Avenue), committing the first $100,000 to the effort. Originally located in "the Bottom," at Peach and Pecan Streets—a historic part of Mobile—the church was moving forward under the leadership of the late Rev. Dr. Howard Johnson. I took great pride in being trusted with significant financial stewardship. At one point, I had hundreds of thousands of dollars at my disposal to help fund the vision. Truevine grew into a multi-million-dollar church, and I had the honor of helping lead that growth with integrity and transparency. It was one of the most meaningful responsibilities of my life.

While Maria and I were building our life together, the country was also going through a significant turning point. The push to establish a national holiday honoring Dr. Martin Luther King Jr. was gaining momentum—but it was far from universally supported. Many in the community resisted the idea, and those who advocated for it, like us, often faced backlash and criticism. It was a time of social tension and growing division, even as we fought to recognize a man who stood for unity and justice.

At the same time, I was achieving major milestones in my professional life. I had become one of the top salespeople in my financial services firm and was honored as a Million Dollar Round Table participant. From the outside, my life may have looked like a series of successes. But beneath that image, I was overwhelmed—trying to meet the demands of a growing family, serve my community, and manage the public expectations that came with success.

Some people assumed that if I sold a million dollars' worth of insurance, I must have been a millionaire myself. The reality was far more complicated. The pressure to live up to those expectations—while balancing national causes, local responsibilities, and family life—began to take its toll. In chasing so many responsibilities, I lost sight of some of the things that mattered most.

During that time, Dr. Lovett and I found ourselves surrounded by mounting negativity. Pressure came from every direction—personally, professionally, and emotionally. I suffered a string of losses: my radio show, my television show, and several properties, including the home I'd kept after my first divorce. But beyond the public fallout, I had to confront a harder truth—I was wrong. I had poured my energy into the community, my career, and public image, but my family often got what was left over. I missed school events. I spread myself too thin. In trying to chase ambition and avoid failure, I failed to protect what mattered most at home.

In the midst of it all, I stepped away from a steady position with my insurance company. My attention was pulled in so many directions—church leadership, hosting two media platforms, managing community projects, and being a husband and father to five children—that I didn't notice what was happening inside my own business. I failed to properly supervise an employee who later got into serious legal trouble. Because I was the one in charge, I took the fall. The questions raised about the business led to the loss of my career and damaged the reputation I had spent years building. The consequences of neglecting the foundation of my professional life came crashing down hard.

The stress took a toll on me mentally and emotionally. I became inconsistent, unfocused—just trying to keep things together, but slowly falling apart. I began drinking more than I should have. Eventually, it caught up with me. I was arrested for DUI, something I never imagined would happen. In that moment, I was ashamed, embarrassed, and unsure of how far things might spiral. I called Attorney James Wilson—my friend, legal counsel, and a judge in Prichard. He advised me not to take any sobriety tests until he arrived. I was released the next day. The experience shook me, but it also forced me to reckon with how far off course my life had drifted.

Dr. Lovett and I wanted to be successful. I failed miserably, and there were problems for her, too. Medicaid was slow to compensate her for treatment rendered. Other doctors refused to treat Medicaid patients, but Maria couldn't turn away poor people in need. Getting paid by the State of Alabama sometimes took four to five months. Some doctors had one day a week set aside for Medicaid patients only. Maria provided services to financially secure individuals with good insurance coverage as well as non-insured patients. Her office had rich and poor scheduled together. The rise in the cost of malpractice insurance for physicians in the State of Alabama and across the country impacted her practice, as well. I owned a company called Access Office Supplies with Marshall Hunt, Sr., Marshall Hunt, Jr., and Rose Young. I was a financial partner more than a working partner. The business began draining my bank account and ultimately failed. A decision had to be made. Life got so bad that we had to leave town and move to another state. Dr. Lovett was offered an excellent opportunity to become a partner in a medical practice by a physician in Columbus, Mississippi. They were going to deliver babies and perform surgeries at the Golden Triangle Hospital. So, with nothing to lose, we made the decision to move to Columbus, Mississippi.

CHAPTER 18

Dinner for Two, Papers for One

The End I Never Saw Coming

I had a new start in Columbus, Mississippi. I was asked to work at Mary Holmes College. One of the blessings during that time was that my son, Alvin Jr. came to live with me, Maria and her three kids. It was a happy time. The kids got along really well. My daughter Brandie stayed behind with her mother.

Unfortunately, Maria became increasingly unhappy with her new business partner. Though they had entered the arrangement as equals, over time she began to feel undermined. He often made executive decisions without her input and began treating her more like an employee than a co-owner. This shift in dynamic made it difficult for her to feel respected or valued in the partnership, and it ultimately created tension that made continuing the professional relationship nearly impossible.

I was involved in a proposal to develop a marina within the city limits of Columbus. The idea was to create a public docking area that would open up economic and recreational opportunities along the waterway—making it more accessible to the surrounding community, especially Black residents who had historically been excluded from such developments.

Working with the People's Minority Council, we organized a coalition that included all the Black doctors in the Columbus area. Together, we applied for government funding to support the project, with the goal of ensuring that the community had both a voice in the planning and a stake in the outcome.

Throughout the process, I collaborated with the office of Alabama Senator Howard Heflin. His guidance and support were instrumental in navigating the government channels. I also received valuable assistance from Helen Carroll, her African American aide, whose insight and advocacy helped us stay aligned with the larger political goals while keeping our community's interests at the forefront.

It was going to be a multi-million-dollar industry and a huge endeavor, including an amusement park. We believed that it would have a tremendous impact on the city and the Northeast Mississippi Region. Nothing like that had ever been done before with an African American group attempting such a large-scale project. We had an opportunity to bid on the project, but the decision went to another group. Of course, we were disappointed after having worked so hard for something that we were sure would be a tremendous success.

That failure knocked us down for a time, but we prayed to God and prepared to get back up again. Certainly, these times tested my faith and had me questioning yet again who I was as a man. But as with all things, the phrase "This too shall pass" continually comforted my spirit and worked patience in my heart.

My life changed as God worked to turn things around. Lord, I thank You! I was able to breathe easily, and the sun was shining brighter. I could see the light at the end of a dark tunnel. At the same time, I tried out a lot of things in my search for the perfect career fit.

I had a chance to acquire a radio station. I also started a radio show at WACR called Live with Lovett. The show became very popular. There was soon an opportunity to work at Mary Holmes

College, and after only one month, I had a chance to become Vice President of Special Affairs. I would create activities and special events that would bring more students to the school.

On one occasion, I created an event that included inviting Mobile, Alabama Judge Cain Kennedy to speak on "Saving a Historically Black University." It helped that Judge Kennedy was married to one of my cousins. All of the activities that went into the event were successful, and the students seemed to thoroughly enjoy it. Many will recall that Cain Kennedy was first elected to serve as an Alabama circuit court judge in 1979. He served from 1979 until he retired in 1998. He made the event a success at a time when I really needed it. I thought I was doing a great job!

It didn't last very long, so I used my education and my Master's Degree to teach school. I was a substitute teacher assigned to work with third graders. The principal made it known that she would observe my class and decide whether or not to keep me. If I could get the students to be attentive when the principal looked in on the class, it would help me. I asked the students to help me out and was confident that they would be in my corner.

Of course, you know what happened next. As soon as the principal came to the door and looked through the window, the kids began running around like crazy! I tried to get them under control, but they went wild, and the principal had a perfect view. At that moment, I gained a respect for teachers that I didn't have before. The right person has to possess a special gift to keep students interested and under control. Much of that gift is acquired through extensive training and experience that I did not have. Even with my 6'5" stature and my loud voice, looking down at them with a hard stare, I could not make those children sit down and behave! They went out of control, and I lost that job. But don't think for a minute that I gave up.

The only thing I seemed to get right was to fail and fail again. I had to take a really hard look at myself in the mirror and ask the questions: "Who am I?" "Why am I failing?" "When will I find success?" "How will I get up again?"

My next move was when I was asked to teach the kids at Lee High School. I replaced a teacher who went on sick leave. So there I was, in charge of a government class — Political Science. I had no idea what I was supposed to do. One of the duties of the job was to manage detention. Was it a coincidence that the worst kids in the school happened to be in my Political Science class?

I couldn't help but think about my Political Science teacher at the University of South Alabama — Mr. Al Stokes. Mr. Stokes had come into my USA life when I was struggling, searching, and needing to get a strong foothold on the correct path for my life. He had certainly done well for himself and, in fact, went on to play a key role in the governance of the City of Mobile under the first Black mayor, Samuel L. Jones. My contact with him taught me to just be present in my circumstances. I would do my best and learn more about myself and my capabilities in the process. That experience helped me to learn something that carried me through the rest of my life.

I stopped being a disciplinarian and let the bad kids know that they were winners. I told them that they could be successful if they put forth a little effort. I promised the students that if they just showed up to my class every day, they already had an A. These were kids who had challenges. Some were great and some were not. I knew that most of them were flunking. I wanted to help them keep the A. If they showed up every day and did nothing, they would end up with a D. If they showed up every day, participated a little, raised a hand, and asked a question, they could at least get a C. I believed that there was good in all of them, even the ones who were known as failures.

It was around 1988 in Mississippi, and we were excited during that time. Jesse Jackson was running for president, and that was big news all over the country. I ventured into owning a poultry farm. We could raise between 50,000 and 100,000 chickens. That did not work. I visited many poultry farms throughout Mississippi. I had extensive training with Tyson Company. They were one of the most successful operations in America. We invested money in it, but the other people we were involved with never came through, so we lost all of our money.

Through all this, we were happy, and there was a lot of joy as we weathered the storms. I knew that we could get through anything. We were strong.

However, the comeback was much harder for Dr. Maria Lovett with her medical career. There were too many issues and challenges. Maria eventually moved to live with her mother in Jackson, Mississippi, because her medical practice was not working well for her in Columbus. Kemba, Enobahkare, and Jumaane went with her. I did not move to Jackson with her. I was still working as an instructor in the school, and Al Jr. was on the basketball team and only had one year left before graduation. However, I traveled back and forth between Columbus and Jackson, intent on keeping my marriage together.

One day, I was pulled over for speeding in Kosciusko, Mississippi. That is the town where Oprah Winfrey was born. I heard that Oprah's family members were living in housing that had been developed and provided to them by Oprah. How I wished Oprah could help me! I needed it while I was taking care of my son. The way I saw it, we were both in the television industry. We both hosted our own shows. It would have been nice to get help, but all I got was a speeding ticket! However, my thoughts were with Oprah as I cruised through her hometown on my way to visit my family.

In Columbus, Mississippi, my son, Alvin Tamar Williams Lovett Jr., became a great basketball player at Lee High School. He inspired me as I weathered the storm of financial trials. Alvin was in my classroom. My money as a substitute teacher was smaller than his, as he made money from the kids, telling them how to get good grades. He taught me what I thought I already knew — that you could reach back and help people.

I met Grady Jones when I first arrived in Columbus, Mississippi (1984/85) with Maria. Grady was married to his first wife. He had a daughter and a stepson. They lived at the end of the block that I moved to, and he was one of the first neighbors to greet me. I wanted to be familiar with the area and the people there. Lots of Black doctors would congregate at our house. We were real friendly people, and everybody liked that about us. You were a guest only once in our home. After that, you were on your own.

Grady Jones was a door-to-door sales insurance agent. He worked a 100-mile radius, including lots of small, rural towns. He was quite successful, and I wanted to know how he did what he did, so we spent a lot of time together. We became like brothers. In the South, they didn't open up to salespeople of color until the late '70s, early '80s. Five hundred dollars bought insurance for an entire family — perhaps seven members — but then only paid out $5,000 if the whole family died. Agents got permission from supervisors to sell some amounts of insurance. I rode with Grady, and he taught me the ropes. He went to church with me and would always say, “No one knows how hard times are unless you tell them. Can’t get help from God without asking.”

Grady was a hero to me. He would die of cancer in the early 2020s. His was a true and pure soul.

Grady Jones was an angel for me. He was a consistent person and a major player in my life. I am not proud that I took our friendship for granted. He never went away through all of the ups and downs of my time in Columbus. Grady visited my home many times. When my wife left to live with her parents, Grady would come with groceries and go into the refrigerator to put food in there while we made drinks and talked. We were both guys who were straight shooters, who supported each other and couldn’t hide problems. We drank Rum & Coke. He would leave the food behind, and that’s what my son and I would eat. Teachers got paid once a month. My money didn’t last. There were days when I didn’t have lunch money for my son. Grady would leave twenty dollars for me, and that’s how I got through the week. I never had to ask for anything from him. He evaluated the situation on his own. Only close friends like him would know that anything was going on in my marriage. His kindness helped me to be a successful parent.

Sometimes Grady took us to different churches. Jerry Rice’s family attended one of them. He was a professional football player with the San Francisco 49ers at that time. Jerry Rice attended Mississippi Valley State University. Alvin was offered a chance to play basketball at Mississippi Valley because of that family relationship.

One night, I was home preparing a candlelight dinner for Maria, who was driving from Jackson to see me. I was preparing to get romantic, so I sent Alvin away for the night to make sure that we had some privacy. Instead of romance and candlelight, it was an ambush. My wife showed up with a lawyer from her mother's church and asked me to sign divorce papers.

It was strange because we never argued about anything. We didn't fight or have any verbal issues. I was immature and didn't understand why I, the great communicator, could not keep a marriage going. Because of this situation, I lost a lot of confidence in myself and just couldn't figure out why I was getting divorced again. I knew that there must be a reason, and I did everything I could to wrap my mind around the reality of my situation. It made no sense to me that I had failed at a second marriage.

It was a heartbreaking experience. Maria's mother, I found out, was prepared to finance Maria's practice by cashing in her own teacher's pension. She must have wanted me away from her daughter with a vengeance. My mother-in-law seemed to push her agenda on Maria. I don't understand why she allowed her mother to manipulate her that way, but I signed the papers and knew that I was doing the right thing.

Unfortunately, Alvin Jr. had a hard time about it. That was a critical step in the process of me spiraling to the bottom. For years after that, I believe that my son felt like he was the cause of our divorce. Of course, that most definitely was not the case. It was 100% my doing — or not doing, as the case may be.

I did my best to protect him from ever feeling any burden. I decided to remain in Columbus until Alvin Jr. graduated from high school. I intensified my focus on being a terrific father to him, instead of to the other children living with their mother. After graduation, Alvin Jr. went off to college in New Orleans, Louisiana. After that, I had no reason to stay in Columbus, so I just went back to Mobile to live with my mother. I was fortunate that I had a place to go. Once again, I was able to start my life over as a newly single man.

CHAPTER 19

From Yankee to Brother

A Story of Faith, Friendship, and Fresh Starts

Starting a new life back in Mobile was not easy. A man named Mark Paul Knutson played a big part in that crucial time of my life. He had recently moved to Daphne, Alabama with his wife, Kim, and his 6-month-old son, Myles. He worked for the American Family Life Assurance Company, now AFLAC. Oather Troldahl ('O. T.') was his boss and took over the regional office in Mobile, with Mark being one of the assistant managers.

When he first arrived at his new job, he noticed something strange. There were thirty white agents and not one black person working for AFLAC in that area of Alabama, where the majority of the community was black. As a former military man and former policeman, Mark realized that people of all colors needed the product. As District Manager, he hired a team of his own. He put ads in local newspapers. I answered the call, walking in with my vast knowledge and background. Mark hired me and broke the color barrier in the process.

The AFLAC National Convention came up in Las Vegas, and Mark had to go. He told me that we would hit the ground running when he got back. I had to make a list of all the business owners I knew. Because of my radio show on WGOK, I already had a lot of contacts. When Mark returned, he kept his word and contacted me. I had a list ready, and he said, "Okay, I'll see you tomorrow."

The first day, we sold three out of the four appointments I had scheduled. When we were back at the office filling out the paperwork, Mark asked how I thought we had done for that day. I thought we did well, but I had no idea how much I could make selling insurance. Mark told me, “You made over $2,000 today.” I had a blank look on my face and then said, “Really?” Mark replied, “Yeah, really. This is what you and I can do down here together, because there's such an opportunity.” With a crazy kind of look on my face, I opened up my folder and slid a paper across the desk. It was an application for another job.

“I got nervous. I just met you, and you're new here. I didn't know if this AFLAC thing was going to work.” Mark looked at it. I had accepted a job at some convenience store to make $800 a month. I told him that I needed the money. Mark said, “I don't think you're gonna need this application anymore.” That was a defining moment that drew us together as a team and as friends.

For the next three months, Mark ran around with me, and his wife, Kim, worked with me sometimes. I took Mark to Donald Duck Day Care Center, which was run by Ellen Marshall. She made history and broke the color barrier, as she became the first black woman to be issued a license to run a day care center in the State of Alabama. Governor George Wallace had to sign off on it.

The company was setting up a Section 125 Payroll tax savings plan. She let us come in and enroll her people. With some of the money we saved on her part of the payroll tax, she turned around and bought $10,000 worth of life insurance for every one of her employees. She won, the employees won, and we sold over $19,000 worth of insurance that day with AFLAC small insurance policies. Kim came in to assist us. She was in one room, and Mark and I were in another. We shuffled the employees in and out all day. After the enrollment, we went back to Mark's house, which was two doors down from his boss, O.T.

We had to get all the paperwork done by the next day because we were in the middle of a contest. We accomplished our goal, made around $9,000 in two hours, and provided the people with great coverage.

If you were high enough in AFLAC sales to win the contest, they sent you a vinyl record with your name on it and invited you to a party at the residence of Paul Amos, who ran AFLAC for a while with his brother, Dan, who was the CEO in 2020. We made it to that elite group and went to the party. Paul's residence was on the 7th floor of the parking ramp where a glass walkway connected over to the 14-story tower of AFLAC. That payroll account that we opened up was AFLAC's seventeenth largest payroll account in Alabama history at that time.

It was impressive how things worked out when Mark and I worked together. Once, while we did paperwork at Mark's home, he offered me something to drink. He drank Miller Light at the time. I wanted vodka and milk. Mark never knew anyone who drank that. He thought it was funny because all he could think about was curdling.

One day, we were working a block away from where our cars were parked. All of a sudden, the sky turned colors. I said, "We need to start jogging right now." Mark asked, "Why do we need to start jogging?" Mark was about to see something that he had never seen before. I started running, and then he started running. We were only halfway down the block when a wall of water came down and drenched us both. We laughed in the car afterwards. The white boy from the North just found out what a Mobile-style monsoon was.

I took Mark to church at the True Vine Baptist Church in Mobile, AL one Sunday. Reverend Howard Johnson was the pastor at that time. I invited Mark to bring Kim and Myles, and Kim's Aunt Sharon, who was visiting. Sharon had recently lost her husband and needed a break. Mark was a little nervous. He had never been to a Southern church before, or a black church. He was going to be meeting my people!

Coming from three generations of Lutheran ministers, he thought it was awesome that the preacher and his wife greeted them at the door. Everyone was so kind to them. They were the only white people in the church, so they stuck out like a sore thumb. I came to get them and they all sat in the second row on the left-hand side. Mark said that he had never been to a church so lively and colorful, with music and flair. He was used to his dad standing in the pulpit, giving a bland, 20-minute sermon, straight out of the Bible. That is a great memory for us. It was a bonding experience. After that, Mark knew that he was in the right place, and with the right guy, at this time in his life.

One day, we were working together and had some free time. I made a phone call, then told Mark to come with me because I wanted him to meet a friend. I took Mark to the projects for the first time. I pointed out where Keith McCants, the great football player from the University of Alabama, used to live. "We're going to see John Tate," I said. Minutes later, we knocked on a door, and a big guy answered. It was my friend, John David Tate. John was a football player who had gone to Jackson State, where he played with Walter Payton. He went on to play for the New York Giants and the Washington Redskins. We entered the house and talked for several minutes.

After a while, Mark looked on the wall and saw a picture of the all-black, All-American team from Jackson State. In the picture, John was standing next to Walter Payton. Mark was amazed that he was standing in front of a real superstar. We all went out in the yard and tossed a football around for a few minutes.

I showed Mark my culture without inhibition. We went to the small restaurants, little shacks on the side of the road, with signs of oyster-eating contests on the wall. One day when we worked together, I took Kim to the location where the last slaves were sold. I showed them the history of my people and shared my life at a time when other people weren't doing that. We took a chance on each other. Mark and I called each other "brother". We showed each other our real lives and overcame prejudice.

Mark and I went to Commonwealth Bank, which I helped to get started. We met with Al Johnson, who ran the bank, to talk about Section 125 payroll. While we were in the meeting, Al Johnson didn't trust what Mark was saying, so he only looked at me. At that moment, I believe that Mark felt the discrimination that I have always felt. Mark said, "You have to sometimes step out on faith with people you wouldn't normally take a chance on." Two different cultures came together to help each other to be something great, despite preconceived notions.

People always asked if Mark was a Yankee or a Damn Yankee. One time, he asked, "What's that?" I told him that a Yankee is a person who's from up North and a Damn Yankee is one who stays here in Alabama. His response was, "Well, I plan on being a Damn Yankee, so get used to it."

Unfortunately, Mark and his family were only in Alabama for three months. Kim was a country girl from a small town in Minnesota.

She had a difficult time working and leaving 6-month-old Myles in daycare. It bothered her because it was very different than what she expected. Mark left to keep his marriage together. Kim would have gone back to Minnesota without him. That's where I initially lost contact with Mark. Later, we connected on Facebook and have kept in touch over the years. I have not seen him since 1992. He let me know that he misses me. I miss him too.

Mark met me when I was at a low point. He gave me a chance and I learned the ropes, selling to people who never had that kind of supplemental coverage on a big scale. He was taking a chance by bringing his young family to Mobile. We both needed something at that time, and fate brought us together to bring each other something good. The bond remained even with a whole lot of time going by. These days, after reconnecting on social media, Mark can check on me every day. He knew me when it wasn't so good, and a lot of life passed us by, but some friendships really do endure despite the passage of time. Myles is now grown, married, and already bought his first house. He is a fifth-grade schoolteacher in Minneapolis. Mark and Kim had a second son, who played three years of football at the University of Minnesota Duluth, and graduated in 2017 with a business degree. Mark and I will always be brothers no matter how much time passes. Sometimes a downfall is a source of our victory. We don't often recognize it at the time. We can have tunnel vision when it comes to all of the negative moments. What we see as a handicap, a financial setback, an emotional setback, or any other kind of setback, is the moment before the comeback. And there is surely a comeback.

My mother and I started a business that we called Dolores and Alvin's Flowers. Her brother came from Los Angeles, California to live with her, temporarily. My uncle's name was Louis Daniel

Williams, who was known as 'Alabama'. I took my nickname from him. He was a very artistic individual. He made beautiful furniture and other unique pieces. His wife was still in Los Angeles. He was getting a new lease on life and was able to help us with the new business. As a team, we decorated people's homes and put flowers in their yards. So, between AFLAC and the flower business, life was great. We were about to be successful again and enjoy a good quality of life.

As one of the top salesman in the region, I won a trip to a Princess Hotel in Mexico, where I met other members of the Amos family, who owned AFLAC. One of the sons got married there, and I stood in the wedding party. Oh, yeah. I was beginning to feel that my success was coming back. However, the good times didn't last. The flower business was not doing well. People didn't want to pay for the work after we finished it. It was not lucrative enough for me. Even though I was still doing well at AFLAC, something was missing. I had an emptiness in my spirit that left me unhappy. All of the things that I loved had gone away. There was no TV show fame, no radio personality recognition, and, sadly, no wife. That spurred in me a decision to start a new life in California. Apparently, there is no limit to how many times a person can regroup and get a fresh start. My goal was to continue on my journey without leaving a big mess behind.

CHAPTER 20

40 Blocks to Forever

The Road to Joyce

It was 1994, and my mother did for me what many other mothers have done for their children. She made a sacrifice to help me with a new beginning. My lovely mother cashed in her diamond ring to give me yet another chance to be a better man. At my Uncle Alabama's urging, she used the money to send me to Los Angeles to get a fresh start. My uncle and his wife lived on 121st Street in the City of Watts, an infamous neighborhood in South Los Angeles. Martin Luther King, Jr. Hospital was nearby.

When I arrived there, I immediately made resumes to send out for a job. I needed to look fresh in preparation for job interviews, so one of my first experiences in my new neighborhood happened when I went to get a haircut near Imperial Highway and Compton Avenue. While on my way home, walking under the 105 Freeway, I was chased by a gang. I was running for my life and didn't know why they were after me. I had just gotten to California, so this large number of young adults had no reason to harm me. I was able to run fast enough at that time to get away without harm. I found out later that it was a dangerous area to be walking in the early evening or after dark. I had no idea that I could get killed walking home at night from a fresh haircut. I asked, "Where am I?" and "What is God doing to me? They wanna kill me."

A while later, I saw Ed Bradley on 60 Minutes and he named the most dangerous places to live in America. He had Nickerson Gardens on the list. My new barber was there and it was close to where I lived. These kids were all wearing red tennis shoes and I thought they were on a high school basketball team. Instead, they were an infamous gang called the Bloods, and they were probably out to do an initiation that night. A move that could easily have gotten me killed that night. I always said that I would keep an eye on the Nickerson Gardens. It wasn't all bad, though. Great singers, like the DeBarge family, came from there. Some people may recall a scene in the movie *Training Day* when Denzel Washington was shot at while driving out of the projects. He had just stolen costly merchandise from a female dope dealer. Nickerson Gardens was like that project.

One day, I was using my expertise as a flower specialist to decorate my uncle and aunt's yard. One of the neighbors came over and invited me to a bid whist party. I accepted the invitation. When I got there, one of the guests was Joyce Ross Eberhardt. She had worked with LAPD in the Southeast precinct at 108th & Main for many years. We got along right away, but when it came time to play cards, neither one of us knew if the other one was any good, but we took a chance and became partners early in the night. We made an excellent team and won every game until we beat everybody in the party.

With all of that expert card playing, I worked up an appetite. Joyce fixed me a plate of delicious food. I liked that, and wondered how she knew that I could eat that much food. I hadn't eaten like that in quite a while, and I ate every bite. We had a great conversation during the evening and eventually exchanged numbers before the night was over. Joyce was also nice enough to let me know that I could go to church with her. I accepted the offer to attend a Sunday service sometime.

Soon after that, Joyce called, and we began to talk every day. I told her that I would come and visit her at her home near 74th

Street and Central Avenue. I lived at 121st and Central. When I was ready to make my move, I walked the entire way, excited to see her. After a short while, I realized that I had strolled for over forty blocks to meet this woman. When I got there, she wasn't even home! Can you believe that? I couldn't believe it myself. I called myself surprising her, but I was the one surprised. I was disappointed after I walked all those blocks. Didn't she know who I was? I was Alvin 'Alabama' Lovett, and she didn't realize it. I was motivated to let her know. And that was the beginning of a new relationship.

I have a big family. Joyce does, too. My mother came from a family of twelve children, and Joyce's grandmother had sixteen children. My Aunt Juanita had sixteen children and one of Joyce's aunts had ten children. That's one of the many things we would come to know that we had in common. As it happened, MANY people would come to know about my '40 Blocks Trek' to see the woman who would complete me. An account of this event was written in an LA paper.

When I went to church with Joyce, we attended the well-known First African Methodist Episcopal Church of Los Angeles. It's the oldest church, founded by African-Americans in Los Angeles, and is now one of the largest churches in the United States. Known as FAME Church, I got star-struck when we saw celebrities, like Dionne Warwick, who was sitting nearby. Players from the Los Angeles Dodgers were there, and there were other famous people. Pat Harvey spoke. She was an anchorwoman who I recognized from the local LA news station. Rev. Cecil Murray was the pastor, and I had never seen so many services. It was nice to witness so many people who were loving the Lord. In Mobile, I never saw more than five hundred people, even at the big churches. But there were several services at FAME in one day, and each one was packed. With all of the celebrities attending, I felt very comfortable and excited about going to that church. That's a good thing for the wrong reason – but true.

When Joyce and I met, there were people who didn't want us to be together. They didn't think that Joyce was worthy of being with me. They didn't even know her, but Joyce heard rumors about people not liking her. Mainly my family. My mother didn't click with her as she felt they should have. Then, while living at my aunt and uncle's, I felt I was treated with a lack of respect. My Uncle Alabama was still in Mobile, living with my mother. People did their best to separate me from Joyce. It was clear to me that nobody cared about me being happy.

At that time, Joyce owned a blue, 1971 Volkswagen that she had for twenty-five years. And if my memory serves me right, that old car was well-kept and clean, but made a lot of noise. She was known for that car. I would have Joyce pick me up on the corner, and not at the house, to avoid her having to deal with any negativity that seemed to surround me. That was not comfortable for either of us. I could be wrong, but I believed there were times when Joyce would be told that I was not at home, even if I was. I feel certain that Joyce was given many reasons why she shouldn't get together with me. I have to say that the very best thing that could have happened for me was that Joyce didn't listen! Our being together was not so much in the cards as in God's plan for our lives.

Joyce had a friend named Laverne who worked with her at the LAPD, and lived next door to me. Joyce would ask her if she'd seen me. Laverne would tell her that I was right outside tending to the yard. Joyce had a discerning spirit that made her cautious and inquisitive. She knew to reach out to someone she totally trusted. The bottom line is that Joyce knew that she was not always getting truthful answers about what was going on with me. Joyce took everything with the proverbial 'grain of salt'. She is a smart woman who examined everything as if it was evidence. It really was evidence that she could trust her feelings about me and herself with me. Laverne was a Shero and an Angel watching over us.

I stayed in touch with my mother back home, and although she sensed I was going through some challenges, I didn't share many details with her. I tried to keep my focus on maintaining peace within my family and navigating my circumstances quietly. I did let her know about the many jobs I had applied for since moving to Los Angeles. With a master's degree in Counselor Education, I applied to positions with the county, the school system, the city—anywhere I thought I could make a difference. But despite my qualifications and efforts, the doors just didn't open. I was discouraged. For all the times I had gone out of my way to help others, it felt like that support wasn't being returned when I needed it most.

Looking back, I realize that I may have expected more than some people were truly able—or willing—to give. Still, I'm grateful. Whatever negativity or indifference others held toward me didn't define my outcome. In the midst of it all, Joyce and I built something strong. Our relationship deepened into a lasting bond that no one could break. For that, I remain deeply thankful for our love lasting for thirty one years and counting.

My father passed away in 1994, leaving behind a significant life insurance policy. He named me executor of his estate, and his wishes were clearly laid out—he wanted specific distributions made to family members, including his brother, sister, my brothers, and others close to him. As straightforward as it seemed on paper, carrying out those instructions was anything but simple. Disagreements quickly surfaced. Not everyone saw eye to eye on how the money should be divided, and the tension was palpable.

The love of money, as they say, can bring out the worst in people—and I saw that firsthand. The negativity in my home grew quickly. Everyone believed their perspective was justified, and perhaps they were, in their own way. But I was caught in the middle. If I leaned toward one person's demands, I'd be compromising my father's clear intentions. I wasn't willing to do that. In the end, the emotional strain and constant conflict made it clear that I couldn't stay in that environment. I made the difficult decision to leave my first California home—and I moved out.

It felt like my own family wanted life to be difficult for me, but nothing worked. Those who tried to ruin my relationship with Joyce had failed. Even at this crossroad that I found myself in, there was nothing that was going to shake us. I chose to do what my father entrusted me to do. Then I moved out.

When I found myself with nowhere else to go, Joyce opened her home to me. It wasn't a decision she made lightly—she was not the kind of woman who let just anyone move into her space. It went against her usual instincts, and I respected her deeply for making that choice. We both knew this was a significant step. Neither of us had ever lived with a partner outside of marriage, and that came with its own weight.

Naturally, I felt the need to contribute—to the household, to the rhythm of daily life, to our growing relationship. Even though the arrangement wasn't part of either of our original plans, we approached it with openness and caution. I had my doubts—quiet questions about whether this was the right move—but nothing in me felt it was wrong. Joyce took a chance on me, and I was determined not to make her regret it.

Living in that neighborhood was good. Joyce was a wonderful woman, and she was such a great cook that I wanted to have food for her when she came home from work. She worked at the police station at 108th and Main, in the Watts precinct, and was ultimately there for 32 years before she retired.

My concern was that I wanted to be productive. I needed to do my part, but I couldn't find a job. One day, I realized that all of the applications and resumes I had submitted had my family's information on them. In fact, they were my references! Knowing that my leaving had probably left a bitter taste in their mouths, I had to include people who would work in my best interest. I updated my resumes and began getting job offers in Los Angeles, but they didn't pay well.

Then I was able to get a job in the movie industry as an extra. I felt good about an opportunity to get back on camera. I worked on a movie called *Strange Days*, starring Angela Bassett. On the set, my natural reporter's instinct kicked in. I worked my way close to Ms. Bassett during a break period. We had a conversation, and in the process, I found myself in violation of the code that says you cannot speak to the stars while on the set. I thought I was a star, too, and that I was an exception. I had a rude awakening and found out that I was not considered a star. I was considered an extra. I discovered there are many levels of stardom.

I was in a situation where I was actually trying to make a

comeback, as thousands of people have done in life. But this was the Big Screen, one closed door away from success. Ms. Bassett was trying to help me and here comes a movie cop to kill my dreams without even knowing me! Was this a time that I fight for an opportunity? Just walk away? When you get this close? I got kicked off the set and had to call Joyce to pick me up. Then I had to tell her that I lost my job as a movie actor. Que Sera, Sera. Whatever will be will be.

Aside from losing my job, I had, once again, lost myself. A thing that I have had to learn, over and over again, is that there will always be people in your life who may speak about whatever you are doing to try to realize your life's goals. They may speak life or death over your situation and circumstances. Your only defense will be prayer. Consistent, fervent prayer will spur you on to your successes in life.

I finally found a position with an agency called IABA, the Institute for Applied Behavior. I was called on to take care of severely, mentally-challenged people, because of my Master's Degree. Many of them were rich people's children. I took care of a young adult named, who I will call, 'Andy'. That's not his name but it protects his anonymity. He was autistic and lived in his own apartment in Brentwood, not far from the home of O. J. and Nicole Simpson. I stayed with him in 24-hour shifts.

It was difficult caring for a young adult with behavioral needs. It brought me down to Earth. Made me humble. My job was to take him places. I had an opportunity to get tickets to events that I otherwise would not have been able to attend. We went to professional games, like the LA Raiders football games, before they moved to Oakland, or the Lakers and Clippers basketball games. I took 'Andy' to the Santa Monica Pier and the 3rd Street

Promenade, both popular spots for celebrities, tourists and regular folks alike.

I began to experience life on a higher socioeconomic level. It was a bit of culture shock to see how the other-half lived. From Watts to Brentwood, it was like night and day. Brentwood was a clean, thriving neighborhood with no obvious social issues. Life was different in Nickerson Gardens. There was a feeling that the area was neglected and had been left to self-destruct in crime and decay. That was fascinating to me.

One day I was walking with 'Andy' in his Dad's Beverly Hills neighborhood. His father drove up and pulled over to us in his car, surprising me. He jumped out and proceeded to give me advice about how to do my job. It got so loud and heated that the person who lived in the house that we stopped in front of called out of his window in an attempt to calm us down. It happened to be a famous actor, Jimmy Stewart. I got to see a legend! What a way to run into a movie star!

There was often something interesting to encounter on our walks. Sometime after that, I got a kick out of seeing James Avery, who played Uncle Phil to Will Smith's *Fresh Prince of Bel Air*. Then there was an unforgettable morning when I was walking with 'Andy' in his Brentwood neighborhood. We happened to come upon the murder scene of Nicole Brown Simpson and Ronald Goldman as the police were conducting their initial investigation. We walked past the gate and saw the bodies covered with sheets and a lot of blood!

Later, at the trial of O. J. Simpson, Joyce was called for jury duty. She was not considered, probably because she worked for the LAPD at that time, and they were involved in the case. This would become the trial of the century and we both brushed up against history.

During that time, in my off periods, I was cooking BBQ in Joyce's yard on 74th Street and Central Avenue. We would take orders and sell BBQ dinners to people in the neighborhood, who were loving the food so much that we launched our first business venture, *Al & Joyce's Catering*. I still had my job as a behavioral counselor, and Joyce was with LAPD. We sold BBQ on the side.

We did tremendous marketing. Joyce's co-workers counted on her good food at every special occasion. We distributed flyers throughout the South Central community and we made good money. People called us, and we delivered. From the money that I made on my job, I bought my first new car, while living in California. I bought a red GEO Metro, from Felix Chevrolet. Joyce loved having a new car to ride in. I did too.

At the peak of our business, I ended up back at the Nickerson Gardens delivering dinners. I was asked to deliver up to fifteen dinners at a time over there. Folks sent young kids to pick up all the food on their bikes and they would take it back to a location. I had no idea what it was all about. Later I was told that I was supplying food to the drug labs for the Bloods gang members.

But they all responded very well to me because Al & Joyce's BBQ had red shirts and I had a red car. I rode around the Nickerson Gardens blasting my Christian music, and they called me 'OG' before I even knew what an 'OG' was. People would say, "Man, you will never go in there and come out alive." But I sold more dinners in Nickerson Gardens than anywhere else. Sometimes they would order two-to-three times a day, fifteen dinners at a time. That's forty-five dinners in a day.

So, we became the dinner suppliers for the guys in the secret locations. As I said before, I had no idea what I was doing at the time, feeding the hardworking people on the drug shifts, but we made good on it. We also had Hispanic gang bangers who bought large amounts of food. We sold lots of BBQ and gained a huge reputation.

When you open a food service business, you do not always know who will request your food. Doing a background check is not what food establishments do. A resume is not required to buy a BBQ dinner. We worked the phone call orders that came in from people who saw our flyers and heard about our good food. We thank God for His Divine Protection, even when we unknowingly worked in a very dangerous environment. There are lessons to be learned from this experience. It has been over 30 years ago. I can still say "Thank You God!"

At my job with the institute that served mentally challenged clients, IABA, I took care of a female patient with twelve different personalities. She said that she had grown up in a cult where bad things happened. Children were abused. Animals, like cats, were cut to drain their blood. They drank the blood. Drugs were given to the kids, along with the animal blood. I found it hard to believe but she swore it was the truth. Before she was able to go to sleep, I was told that I had to say goodnight to each of the twelve personalities, and call them by name. She said that is how they were comforted.

One night, there was a personality who opened her eyes back up after I called that name, and she said that she was going to get a knife and stick me as soon as she saw me fall asleep. I called the agency and told them that I could not stay the rest of that night, and they would have to send a relief person. After they sent a replacement, I left and never went back to work with mentally challenged people again.

Months later, there came more hardship as some people came to Joyce's house and told us that we had to move because the rented house was in foreclosure. They said the house had been in foreclosure for a while, and the old landlord was still collecting the rent from us.

We got put out and moved to Compton. One Sunday morning, we called FAME Church and asked them to pick us up. Our car was not running, and we still wanted to attend. They called back to say that they didn't serve Compton.

So, we ended up in a church called New Philadelphia A.M.E. They began with 27 members and grew to nearly 3,000 members. Pastor Sherman Gardner, a young fellow from Mississippi, led the church. Joyce and I were the church cooks for some occasions.

It may be an overstatement, but I like to say that Joyce and I had a lot to do with the growth of that church's attendance. It made me feel good that we had a ministry. After the service, we had snacks for the people to eat while they were heading to their cars.

We cooked for as many as 3,000 people at one time, so our business was booming and prosperous. That followed a time in our lives that wasn't so bright, but I had been through worse. We chose to fight together to make our lives what we dreamed they could be.

I'm happy to say that the new relationship with Joyce Ross Eberhardt turned into a happy marriage with my soulmate, one that I still enjoy to this very day.

CHAPTER 21

The Shootout at the Los Angeles Times

How Sales, PTSD, and God Rewrote My Story

I began working at the *Los Angeles Times* call center on Cashdan Street in Carson, California. Our team was responsible for calling potential subscribers and encouraging them to sign up for newspaper delivery. I quickly became one of the top salespeople in the department. I had a natural talent for phone conversations—building rapport, understanding people's needs, and closing the deal. I consistently led in sales, bringing in more subscriptions than anyone else on the floor. With that success, the income started to improve.

At the same time, Joyce and I began building something of our own. We started selling homemade peach cobblers, and they quickly gained popularity. Before long, we had our cobblers placed in local grocery stores and restaurants. On payday weekends, we also sold homemade dinners—another steady source of income. Between the call center job and our side business, we found our footing in Carson and made a good life for ourselves. Our daily sales goal was to sell over 800,000 newspapers. We had to sell 1.5 million Sunday only papers.

I developed a strong bond with many of my co-workers, especially those who were struggling to make sales. I'd often step in, take their headsets, and demonstrate how to close a deal—just so they could earn a paycheck. Over time, they started using the techniques I shared and began to succeed on their own. Helping them gave me a sense of purpose, and many of those people remain my friends to this day.

The call center attracted people from all walks of life, including aspiring artists and entertainers. One of them was a young D. L. Hughley, who worked alongside us before his rise to fame. He became one of the kings of comedy alongside, Bernie Mac, Steve Harvey, Cedric The Entertainer. Even then, he had a sharp wit and charisma that stood out. Looking back, it was remarkable to share space with someone who would go on to make such a cultural impact.

I used to carpool to work with a retired white police officer named Steve and an African-American Vietnam veteran named James. We all worked at the call center together, but James had been struggling. He wasn't making enough sales to cover his rent and was facing eviction. On top of that, some of our co-workers began teasing him about his performance, which only added to his frustration.

Then one day, everything changed.

James came to work with a gun hidden in his backpack. Without warning, he pulled it out and shot a colleague named Washington—originally from D.C. Blood splattered everywhere, including on me. Then James turned the gun on me. I froze as he raised it to my head and pulled the trigger—once, twice, three times. Click. Click. Click.

There was no second shot. The first had fired, but the next three misfired or jammed. In that moment, I believed I was going to die. My body shut down. I couldn't move, think, or speak. I was face to face with death—and I broke.

When I realized James wasn't firing anymore, I bolted from the building in sheer panic. I ran without direction, dazed and covered in blood. I spotted a city bus about to pull away and jumped on board. I pleaded with the driver to take me off the regular route, explaining through trembling words that there had just been a shooting. I must have looked like a suspect. Bloodied shirt. Shock in my eyes. And now, helicopters buzzed above and police cars raced through the streets.

Eventually, I found myself in an unfamiliar neighborhood and ended up in a garage where a group of squatters had set up an old television powered by an extension cord. They were watching the news, and there it was—my workplace, the crime scene. I sank into a corner, numb and disoriented, a half-gallon of vodka resting beside me. The newscaster reported that after the shooting, James had walked into another room and taken his own life.

I didn't see it happen, so I can't confirm if it was true. But that's the story I heard. And by the end of that day, James was dead.

I didn't know the people in that vacant house, and I still don't know how I ended up there. I don't remember getting the half-gallon of vodka. I don't know if I got off the bus on my own or if someone helped me, or whether I ever changed out of the bloody, soiled clothes. My memory from that time is fragmented at best—large parts of it are completely blank. I was disoriented, disconnected from reality, and moving through the day as if on autopilot.

Looking back, I realize I wasn't functioning in any normal sense. I was broken—mentally, emotionally, and spiritually. And yet, something carried me through. I truly believe it was divine intervention. In that moment of total disconnection, it was not my own strength guiding me forward. It was God. I was lost, but I wasn't alone.

After the shooting incident, I was diagnosed with PTSD and began psychiatric treatment to process the trauma. The event had left a deep mark on me, mentally and emotionally. During my recovery, I continued working at the *LA Times*, determined to hold on to some sense of structure and purpose. For seven years, I stayed committed to both my healing and my job, slowly regaining confidence in myself.

As part of that process, I immersed myself in the printed word. I read every major newspaper available—*The LA Times*, *The Orange County Register*, *The Press-Enterprise*, and others that covered Long Beach, Ventura, and the Inland Empire. I used that knowledge not only to stay informed, but to sharpen my skills as a salesman. What truly set me apart, though, was how I combined that knowledge with my background in financial planning.

I spoke to customers not just as a sales rep, but as someone genuinely offering value. I showed them how to use every section of the paper—from finance to classifieds—to improve their lives. I'd say, "Give it eight weeks. If you don't like it, you don't have to keep it." Almost everyone gave it a try. I taught them how to use grocery coupons to save real money, and people appreciated that. I made over 200 calls per shift and became one of the top performers in the department.

Eventually, the job came to an end when the department shut down. But it had been a meaningful chapter—one where I not only rebuilt my sense of self but proved that I still had the voice, discipline, and determination to succeed.

CHAPTER 22

Everybody Is Somebody

How the Streets of Compton Taught Me to Love Like God

By the early 2000s, I had lost direction. My goals no longer felt clear, and I found myself drifting—emotionally numb and untethered from the life I had once worked so hard to build. During that time, I began spending more of my days with people I never would have imagined myself around years earlier. Many were struggling—homeless, broken, overlooked by society. Some had criminal pasts. Others battled addiction or carried visible scars from lives of hardship.

Yet strangely, I found a kind of comfort in their company. There was no judgment, no need to pretend. In a world where I felt like I had failed, they accepted me without conditions. I was still drinking heavily and relying on medication for my PTSD, but something about those connections kept me grounded. I began to see the humanity in people others might write off—their stories, their pain, their resilience. That time changed me. It made me want to reach out, to help anyone I could, for as long as I'm given the chance to do so.

During a difficult chapter in my life, I spent a lot of time on the streets of Compton—drifting, disconnected, and often in the company of people many would dismiss or ignore. But one moment reminded me just how easily judgment can cloud our understanding of worth.

One day, I was crossing Alondra Boulevard at Central Avenue when a man named Tennessee sitting at the bus stop suddenly shouted, "Run!" I turned just in time to see a car speeding toward me. I barely moved out of the way in time to avoid being hit. When I looked back to see who had warned me, I realized it was a man I had seen around the neighborhood—a regular on the corner, known by many as a drunk who claimed to be B.B. King's cousin.B.B. King (born Riley B. King, September 16, 1925 – May 14, 2015) was an iconic American blues guitarist, singer, and songwriter. His guitar, famously named "Lucille", became a symbol of his sound.

People often looked right past him. But that day, he saw me. He cared enough to speak up—and in doing so, he may have saved my life. That moment stayed with me. It reminded me that worth isn't always wrapped in clean clothes or a steady job. Sometimes the very people we're taught to overlook are the ones who show us the most humanity.

During this period, I returned to FAME Church, one of the largest and most influential churches in Los Angeles. I sought spiritual grounding and began receiving counseling from Rev. Cecil Murray, the senior pastor. Despite those efforts, I was still in the midst of a serious downward spiral. My life lacked stability, and I found myself once again searching for work. But instead of staying focused on rebuilding, I began spending more time on the streets, surrounded by people battling their own addictions.

One afternoon, that lifestyle caught up with me. I was out with a group when Compton Sheriff's deputies pulled up on us. They found crack pipes and other drug paraphernalia on the ground. The others admitted the items were theirs, but when the officers pressured me to claim the same, I refused—because they weren't mine. Still, they arrested me along with the rest. That day taught me a hard lesson: proximity can carry consequences, even if you're not the one holding the evidence.

At the time, the Compton Sheriff's Department had just taken over policing duties from the city's own department. With the new contract came a mandate to restructure and crack down on crime. Compton was gaining national attention as one of the most violent cities in America, and the response was aggressive: large-scale raids, mass arrests, and a focus on Black men in public spaces. It was less about justice and more about control.

That day, I didn't look like someone with privilege or protection. I didn't look like a Kennedy, a Bush, or a Trump. My degrees and professional background meant nothing. The deputies weren't interested in who I was—only how I looked and where I happened to be standing.

The regulars on the street knew how to navigate situations like this. Some admitted ownership of the drug paraphernalia, knowing it would likely get them a quick release. I told the truth—it wasn't mine—but that made me the odd man out. Law enforcement didn't like losing control of the narrative. If they couldn't make sense of your story or force it to fit, they assumed you were lying. So they cuffed me and put me in the squad car.

That's when I learned something painful: sometimes, telling the truth won't protect you. In fact, it can make you more of a target when the system is already set up not to believe you.

I'm not one who runs from my truths. I did try crack when it was presented to me. Several times, actually, but I preferred the alcohol. I was a drunk, so the crack was not my drug of choice. I admit that I found comfort in hearing other people's stories and about their experiences with drugs. Young people, mothers, and all kinds of people who would do anything to get that drug and get that fix. From being a trained counselor, I had first-hand experience and knowledge of what leads people to go off a cliff into another space where they can't come back. It was a learning experience for me to have been in that environment of people. It taught me compassion and understanding for the addicts. If human beings can accept that we all have flaws, and accept other human beings as being flawed, then we can begin to see each other with the same love that God sees us. We can forgive ourselves and each other, and learn to become better.

In the end, I was charged with possession of drug paraphernalia and forced to go to Narcotics Anonymous and Alcoholics Anonymous classes. I was ashamed of what happened to me and how far I had fallen away from who I thought myself to be. And I didn't want Joyce to know, but there was no way to completely hide the circumstances from her. It would be twelve years later, before Joyce found out that this happened. My heart had no respect for the court's decision because I felt like they wanted to make an example of me. I wasn't a drug addict, as I saw people in my environment, so I stopped going to the classes. I didn't think I needed them. The truth is, I probably did need the AA classes, because I was a bona fide drunk, but I wasn't a drug addict. They held the two classes at the same time.

I couldn't afford to miss work, so I skipped them both. That wasn't a smart decision, because the possession charge remained on my record, in spite of the policing politics that were so clear to everyone! It was an eye-opening moment when I figured out that there are a lot of people with criminal records who are not criminals. It was commonly said by many people in Compton that the Sheriff's Department would stop hundreds of black males without cause, just to see if they had existing warrants. This was how they proposed to reduce crime in Compton. Non-criminals had to suffer from this twisted policing policy. Even today, parents still have to teach their boys about this.

After a careful and fair review of the incident and the flawed policing practices surrounding it, the charges against me were ultimately dismissed. The review process examined not only the circumstances of my arrest but also the broader pattern of law enforcement misconduct that had come to light in Compton. The case did not hold up under scrutiny—there was no credible evidence, and the truth was finally acknowledged.

Being able to share this experience means a great deal to me, especially with young people and parents who may not always see how quickly life can change. Bad things do happen to good people. Sometimes, just being in the wrong place at the wrong time is enough to alter your path.

But setbacks don't have to be the end of the story. What matters most is how you rise after the fall. My record was cleared, my dignity restored, and the journey I walked became part of the testimony I offer to others. I was later recognized by the City of Compton and honored by the Compton Historical Society for my community service in Southern California. That recognition meant more to me than any headline or title—it reminded me that redemption is possible, and that truth, in time, can prevail.

After the charges were cleared and my name restored, I knew I needed stability—something steady to ground me again. That opportunity came when I was hired at the Sears Call Center in the Carson Mall. The job wasn't glamorous, but it was consistent, and it gave me a way to rebuild my confidence.

I worked in the Warranty Department, where we called customers across the country to offer extended coverage on their purchases. We started early with East Coast calls, moved through the Midwest, and wrapped the day with the West Coast. With the skills I'd honed at the LA Times and my natural gift for connecting with people, I quickly stood out as one of the top salespeople on the team.

Though the department was eventually closed and our work outsourced overseas, the experience marked an important chapter in my recovery. It reminded me that no matter what I'd lost, I still had the ability to rebuild—one conversation at a time.

CHAPTER 23

Between Katrina and Compton

Saving Others While Losing Myself

In August 2005, Hurricane Katrina devastated the Gulf Coast, striking cities like New Orleans and my hometown of Mobile, Alabama. The destruction was widespread and overwhelming. In the aftermath, I received a call asking me to return to Mobile to assist the survivors. Before moving to California, I had been one of the first African-American State Farm Insurance agents in Alabama. I had built strong relationships across the region, ensuring hundreds of churches and thousands of families. That background made me uniquely positioned to help people recover—guiding them through the process of securing insurance claims and rebuilding their homes and lives.

One of my most significant contributions during my time with State Farm was helping to amend fire policies to include replacement cost coverage. This change allowed policyholders to replace homes and buildings at current market value, regardless of depreciation—a vital protection for families facing catastrophic loss. At the time, Black homeowners were often overlooked or underserved by insurance companies. Many local agents focused on white neighborhoods and churches, leaving Black communities without adequate coverage. I worked to change that by ensuring their claims were filed properly and that they received fair treatment. Discrimination in the insurance industry was—and in many ways still is—a painful reality, but I did everything I could to advocate for my community and help people recover more quickly after natural disasters.

Returning to Mobile came at a time when I desperately needed a reset, even if no one around me realized it. I was still battling depression, struggling with PTSD, and drinking heavily. I was not the same Alvin who had once left Mobile full of ambition and direction. Key parts of my identity—my confidence, my discipline, my sense of purpose—had faded.

But I made a decision. I got a haircut, brushed my teeth, put on a suit, and went home to stay with my mother. There was work to do. My knowledge and experience in insurance were needed, especially in the wake of Hurricane Katrina. People were dealing with loss and uncertainty, and I found that helping them helped me, too. I began hosting seminars in churches, guiding families through recovery, and offering support to local businesses trying to rebuild. In the midst of all that chaos, I started to feel something shift. Even though I hadn't yet healed myself, I was still able to make a difference in the lives of others—and that gave me a reason to keep going.

After three months of being in Mobile, Joyce called me. She asked when I was coming back to Compton. We were in danger of losing our home—three months behind on the mortgage—and facing eviction. That conversation hit me hard. Up to that point, I had been pouring myself into recovery work, offering my skills to help others rebuild after Hurricane Katrina. But it hadn't occurred to me that my work was completely voluntary, and that I wasn't bringing home a paycheck. I had lost track of time, and of my responsibilities at home.

That phone call forced me to face something deeper. As much as I believed I was finding purpose again, I had also been avoiding what mattered most—my commitment to Joyce and our life together. I realized how much I had let her down. In that moment,

I made a vow: to be a good husband, a better man, and the person I was always meant to become. With renewed determination, I decided it was time to return to Compton.

CHAPTER 24

Making 'Car Pros Kia' One of the World's Best

Grit, Giving, and Global Growth

My new life began when I returned to Compton in 2006, but it wasn't easy. I needed a job that could save Joyce and me from being evicted. I needed to work where there was a retirement plan. I considered the school system, the county, the city, and the post office. All of the processes were going to take too long. To teach school, I would have to take (and pass) an educator assessment for the State of California, that is the Basic Educational Skills Test (CBEST). Unfortunately, that was not an option. I didn't have time to go back to school, not with all of the advanced degrees that I already had.

After considering all of my job options, I came into a new realization and opened my mind to a whole new possibility. I went into a full job-hunting mode. Going through the newspaper one morning, I ran across something in the want ads that revealed that car salesmen could get six-figure incomes. I didn't have a car, so I hopped on a bus and decided to go to the Car Pros Chrysler Jeep dealership at Avalon and the 405 Freeway because that was the first car lot that I saw. It was the old Don Kott Ford 'Super Dealer' dealership, which was the mecca of car sales for years. The dealership was being closed. The Ford Motor Company dropped its Carson franchise, which was being run by Sonic Automotive Inc., and they sold the dealership to Ken Phillips and Car Pros Chrysler Jeep.

In 2007, Leonard Fischer worked as a top salesman at Car Pros Chrysler Jeep. He was in the number one spot almost every month. Early one morning, he was watching the floor as I strolled up and walked in, slightly hunched over and dressed in a bad suit. I walked up to Leonard, who appeared to be in charge, and asked, “Are you guys hiring? I'm looking for a job.” Leonard looked at me, knowing that I didn't fit the profile of someone who was working as a salesman in that business. He asked, “You wanna be a salesman?” I looked him in the eye and said, “Yeah, I'm looking to be a salesman.” Leonard scratched his head a little bit and explained that they were only hiring experienced car dealers to work for them. The company had recently changed ownership and they were not interested in taking chances on somebody like me. They only wanted salesmen who could make a lot of money for them. Even so, I appreciated that he took a little extra time to talk to me. In a five-minute conversation, he saw something about me that inspired him. Later he told me that I looked like I needed a real chance. He was right. I needed even more than that. I needed a miracle, and something about the whole scenario made him decide that he wanted to help. He asked me a few more questions. I didn't give the answers that he expected. Leonard went inside another office to talk to management. They looked out and immediately decided that they weren't interested in hiring me. With a little light pleading, they agreed to let Leonard give me an application that I was asked to fill out and bring back. I did what they asked, but when I turned in my application, their position was clear. “Why, Leonard? Look at the guy! We're not hiring him.”

When I got home, and before I had a chance to say a word to Joyce, she told me that we were going to be put out on the street in a matter of hours. Then she asked me how the interview went at the dealership, and the first thing that came to mind was that I needed to tell her a lie. I told her that I thought they liked me at the car lot and I even put a little bit more butter on that toast by saying I had a second interview. There would be an eviction, and I couldn't tell her. All I could do was go back and change the outcome. I didn't have any more bus fare and didn't have any money. I asked a couple of the corner drunks if they had bus tokens. They always seemed to have extra tokens from the welfare office. A couple of guys helped me out, and I took the bus back to Car Pros. When I got off the bus, I had to walk 1/2 mile to the dealership. It was no big deal. It gave me time to think. During that walk, I decided that I could not afford for them to tell me no a second time. So, when I got back to the lot, I immediately started talking to customers. The other salesmen noticed that I was having conversations with people entering the dealership and immediately called Ken Phillips, who was the owner. They told him that they had a guy out there talking to customers and that they wanted to call the police. Ken asked them why, and they said, "Because the guy thinks he works here. He must have some kind of mental issues, or maybe he's on drugs." Ken didn't want to have the police there at that time. He had his reasons, so he suggested that they have me fill out the application again, and also take a drug test, which should get rid of me. They did all of that and I passed, so they had no reason to let me go.

I thank God that Leonard Fischer didn't give up so easily. After much prodding from him, and a man from Ghana named Christopher Owusu, who yelled out for them to give me a chance, they finally said, "Fine, Leonard. If you think we should hire him, then he's your project." Leonard was about to be promoted. He had power, and management listened to him, so they decided to hire me. They gave me a chance and allowed me to be the only person there to sell cars without any previous experience. A stranger went out of his way to help me. It was a blessing.

Without his support, they would not have hired me, but Leonard saw that I needed a break. He wanted to be the one to give it to me. Another stranger, Christopher Owusu of Ghana, West Africa, cheered me on. Both men showed heroism that completely changed my life and lifted me up to a place of salvation and success. Both were Heroes in my life.

As a top State Farm Insurance salesman, I insured thousands of cars, but I didn't know any details about my newest product. However, I taught myself a lot of information by going onto the lot and reading the labels on each car. I kept learning about the products and the selling points. I gained a lot of knowledge, but there was one huge problem. At the time that I was hired, Ken Phillips was a new car dealership owner with no heavy traffic coming to the store, at the time that I was hired. It concerned me when I realized that I had no customers. How was I supposed to save Joyce and me from becoming homeless if nobody came to buy cars? Because of Leonard's faith in me, I tried to do my best every day. I was not a young man anymore. There were adjustments to be made. I needed to tighten up on the dress code and really clean up my act, but I needed money badly. Leonard did his best to show me the ropes, but I was dizzy from working on the lot. A few days in, I confessed to Leonard that all of the cars looked the same. I honestly couldn't tell one car from another. That would make me a bad car salesman. But I was Leonard's project, and he was not about to fail. He didn't give up on himself, and he didn't give up on me. He took me under his wing, gave me complete knowledge of the vehicles, and taught me the process. I soaked it all in. Leonard was my mentor, and I can call him a Hero. I thought, "He must have a battery in his back, like the energizer bunny. How do I catch up with this guy? He moves fast. He's running here and there. When he gets a customer, he sells them a car. I gotta be like that!"

By the third or fourth month, I had taken all of the knowledge that Leonard gave me and turned everything upside down. I beat him, by one car, to become "Salesman of the Month." I accomplished that feat in a short time frame, and Leonard was happy for me. I was grateful and very thankful for everything he did for me. He kept telling me that I did it, not him. My response was, "You're the only one who believed in me, man. Nobody else would give me a chance. I don't know how to repay you." His reply was simple. "Just keep doin' what you're doin', man." Leonard soon moved into the Finance Department and handed the sales baton over to me. I was the top salesman almost every month. I was consistent. I implemented some of my ideas and started putting out flyers. I gave the folks who were hanging out at the neighborhood liquor stores a few assignments, and I offered to put a little change in their pockets. The dealership was against that practice and tried to shut me down. They wanted me to get approval and not ruin the reputation of the dealership. By this time, Leonard was in upper management and was able to use his leverage. He fought side-by-side with me to convince everyone at the dealership that it was in their best interest to let me do what I was doing to bring in customers. Management loosened up a bit, and we got the dealership to agree with my methods, once they realized that they were also going to benefit. Although they still tried to control the content of my flyers, at least they let me spend my own money to advertise myself and the dealership. People began coming into the dealership with the flyers that were being passed out on my behalf, and the other salesmen began (shall I say) "acquiring" my customers. That means that the company was being fed off of my efforts and I wasn't even getting credit. Those shady salesmen were greedy and scandalous. There was no respect for me and the new business that I brought in. I needed to find a way to control the situation. I wanted to show how much my efforts were working for the company.

While I was at work one day, I noticed that there was a sales incentive. If someone came to the store and asked for a specific salesman, they would get ten dollars. I asked the manager if I could leave to find customers. It was an unusual request, so they didn't know what to think about me. They might have thought I was going to get drugs or do something else shady. I was stepping out of the box, being contrary to the method that they used to sell cars. They said that people didn't do that. Salesmen stayed on the lot and waited for people to come, and then they sold them a car. Well, I couldn't wait, so I had to be creative. And I had to do it quickly. I left the lot and went down the street to the mall. Sears Department Store was there. When I used to work there, nearly a hundred people went in and out of the employee lunchroom during its busy time. I went there to make an announcement. There was at least a hundred people there at the time. I pleaded my case and told them about my dilemma. "All you have to do is go to Car Pros Chrysler and ask for 'Alabama'. That will help me out." They were not obligated to buy anything, but that ten dollars from each person who went there would add up and do a lot to keep me from losing my house.

After that, I went to all the stores in the mall and made the same pitch to each store and to anyone who would listen. I told them the truth. I told them that I was about to be homeless, but that I just got a job at Car Pros Chrysler and I needed their help. Soon after that, the Ken Phillips store was full of potential customers asking for me. My efforts had a significant impact on the flow of people who flocked in there like never before. The other salesmen had never seen anything like it. When I wasn't there, they continued to take a lot of my customers. I discovered that the car sales business was cutthroat, although there were some guys who sold cars on my behalf and split the commission with me. Joyce and I were able to save our house and, as far as I was concerned, a whole new career began for me. There was something about bouncing back from a bad period in my life that made me very humble. It wasn't long before I realized that my opportunity wasn't only for me. I was very pro-black, and I had a vision of how to put poor people into cars. They lived in sub-standard communities with extremely limited finances and opportunities. There were young mothers on the bus with their kids. Leonard gave me an opportunity, and I wanted to pass it on. I wanted to help them buy cars. It wasn't all about making money or being the top guy. It was about the community, which was the motivation to my salvation.

I met Calvin Cook in 2007. I knew his brother, 'Green Eyes', but I didn't know him. My mother was sick, and she was in Compton with us. Green Eyes sent me a card. She was doing better, so I went by to let him know that I appreciated him sending the card. When Calvin opened the door, and I asked for Green Eyes, he told me that he was the older brother. I said, "Green Eyes has an older brother? I didn't know that." A lot of my friends didn't know that Green Eyes had a brother who was 13 years older than him. In 1953, when Green Eyes turned five years old, Calvin said he was home from the Navy on Christmas leave. I laughed and wanted to know how old he was. He told me that he was as old as Methuselah. I decided to leave and said that I would catch up with Green Eyes later. A few weeks went by, and I ended up talking to Calvin again. He was retired and talked about the fact that he was taking care of his mother, whose health was good at that time. My mother, Dolores, was seeing a couple of doctors and needed to get to her appointments. Since Joyce was working at the police department, and I was working, too, Calvin offered to take my mother to her doctor appointments.

When Calvin met my mom, Ms. Dolores Williams, he picked her up in his Expedition! They hit it off well. He loved poetry and shared some of it with her. He said it was just like Morgan Freeman and Jessica Tandy in Driving Miss Daisy. They laughed and talked, going here and there. Sometimes they went to a restaurant to eat lunch. Wherever she wanted to go, and whatever she wanted to do, Calvin was there to accommodate her. He was happy to do it, and I appreciated him. He did the same thing for his mom, and my mother became his second mom. They had a good time together.

Eventually, my mother went back to Mobile. Calvin stayed in touch with me, and our friendship grew closer and closer. He told me that he was a certified locksmith. However, he shared with me that he had gone through a divorce, years before, and his wife shredded everything of importance, including his certificates. One day I needed to get my locks changed. Calvin told me that he would help me without charging an arm and a leg. He would only do it for friends because he didn't have a certificate anymore. He said, "I can't go picking people's locks and have the man walk up and ask for my credentials, because I'd be going straight to jail. I'm retired from the Navy. This ain't gonna work." Calvin and I talked and laughed together often. It was like we were twins. He would say, "This is Alvin, and I'm Calvin." We looked somewhat alike and, if you talked to people long enough, they tended to believe you. But, it was funny because I'm 6' 6" and he's 5'4" and he continued to play it off. We had to remind people that not all twins are identical. We had it going on. At the writing of this book Alabama Buttermilk, I have reached 71 years of age and Calvin Cook, another Hero in my life, is almost 90 years old. Both, living on grace.

When my friend Calvin needed a car, he came and bought one from me. It was a Chrysler 300 that he kept for 33 days. He was told to bring it back because of the money that he was paying for alimony. They were taking half of his Navy retirement and said it messed with his income. He brought the car back in the morning. We asked if he had put any miles on it. He said that it was a few, but Calvin had taken that car everywhere and ended up with 1,900 miles on it! If he thought of somewhere to go, he went. His friends were impressed that he finally got the car he wanted. A year later, Calvin got another car from me that didn't work out. He eventually ended up buying a 2013 Kia Soul that he kept during the time that my mom was sick in the hospital. He would go to see Mama Dolores, as he called her, and write and read religious poems to her. It made her feel a whole lot better. He stayed with her, in and out of the hospital, for the rest of her life. And even though there was early drama between Joyce and my mother, Joyce called her often before she died, and they were good with each other in the end.

The last part of my mother's life was in Southern California with me and Joyce. She had a lot of health issues, so we brought her to live with us and we cared for her until her death in a hospice facility in Gardena, California on April 29, 2015. Meanwhile, Joyce retired from the Los Angeles Police Department and Calvin came to the retirement ceremony, which was really nice. It was a Los Angeles Police Department retirement for Joyce, after thirty-two years of dedicated service. Joyce did all of those years in the Southeast Community Police Station, Precinct 18. The Southeast Police Station served the neighborhoods of Athens Park, Harbor Gateway, Jordan Downs, Nickerson Gardens, San

Miguel and Watts. All of those areas were under the jurisdiction of the South Bureau. The retirement ceremony took place at The Proud Bird Food Bazaar and Events Center near LAX Airport. It was a grand affair but I think everyone would have liked it better if Joyce had prepared the food!

Since Calvin's mom passed away at the age of 98, he had been living in Hesperia, California. His ex-wife told him that if he acted right, he could come back, so he agreed. Calvin and Green Eyes were brothers but they were not very close, although things have gotten better since their mother passed. Calvin is still very close to me. We get along great and he has a similar sense of humor. If I want to do something or go somewhere, he's ready to hang out. Best of all is when he can catch me by surprise. For instance, he'll ask me to stop by his house. When I get there, he'll have half gallons of different kinds of alcohol. It just perked me up! Calvin would also get Patron tequila for Joyce. He was getting the liquor at 1/3 the price and would buy ten or fifteen bottles at a time. He's had close to fifty bottles of alcohol in his house on any given day, fifths and half gallons.

Calvin's a drinker and liked Schlitz Malt Liquor and vodka. At Christmastime, he became an eggnog lover. He would get a tall glass, fill it with half eggnog and half milk, and then sip on it and drink nothing else for days. Calvin told the story of the last time he was drunk. According to Calvin, it was in 1959 at a wine festival in Athens, Greece and he hasn't been drunk since. He said that it took him three days to be able to eat again, so he vowed never to let that happen again. He's not a big person, but he likes to eat. Breakfast was his most important meal. He would often call me and offer to treat me to breakfast at Denny's, and we would hang out. Those are fond memories of Compton California.

I quickly became a top salesman at the Chrysler store without knowing much. I began to have so many customers coming to the store that it caught the attention of Ken Phillips, the owner, whose office was next to mine. He had taken me under his wing to train me so that I could get better – and I did. He wanted me to be like he was when he got started – and I believe I was. He told me a story about how he helped students in the Washington area, and then gave back to those schools, and got repeat customers. That's how he became a top salesman and was able to buy his own dealership.

Ken's story inspired me to work with the schools in Compton and give back to help the students. The deal was that if you bought a car from Alabama', you would get a discount and Car Pros would also contribute to your school. That was the beginning of the Compton 'Alabama' Discount Plan. That program became a primary source of success for the Car Pros Chrysler Jeep dealership. Through this discount plan, I would sell cars at a discount and then donate $100 of my commission to the city of Compton for youth programs and the needy.

A lady who was part of an organization called His Sheltering Arms, came by one day and said that they needed a van to pick up the homeless women and children in Watts. She asked if I could donate one. I asked the owner of the dealership if there was a van to offer. He said, "No, we're in business to make money, not to give away vehicles." He assured me that they could purchase one if they chose to, but they would not get one for free. Other salesmen told me that I had twisted my thinking. Then, one day, the good Lord sent a white soldier who had just returned from Desert Storm. He had a van to trade in because he wanted to buy a new one. I told him that I had two brothers who were in the military, and both had served in Vietnam. I told him about my oldest brother, Britt Mose Lovett, Jr., who had served in the United States Marine Corps and our middle brother, LaGrand who was a United States Army Ranger. He heard that both of my brothers were no longer living but they had served this nation with distinction. He also heard that I would not have a veteran pay full price for what was being charged for those vans. I discounted the new van for him, and he offered to give me the one that he was trading in. I turned him down and told him to keep the trade-in, and I would still discount him. After he left with the new van, I found out that he had signed the pink slip for the old van over to me without my knowledge! I thought it was a trick! White people used to do things like that to black people down south. Fool them into taking possession of something that they could get in trouble or arrested for. I wasn't about to lose my job, so I told Ken Phillips that this customer had signed over the pink slip to his van. Ken told me it was mine if the man gave it to me. I immediately accepted the blessing and brought the van to some mechanics. They refurbished it, repaired the van, and made it look like new. Then I donated the van to His Sheltering Arms and they continued to serve the community - eight years and counting. They transported homeless women and children in Watts, who had no place to go. I felt really good about that.

After that, I helped other groups - Justice for Murdered Children, Helping Youth Through Golf, Compton Chamber of Commerce. I made sure that students had computers to study at the Compton Airport and paid for students to learn to fly airplanes. 'I Believe I Can Fly' became more than just lyrics to a song! I was honored to be able to finance concerts and feed the homeless in Compton and Los Angeles.

In 20016, I worked with tennis stars, Venus and Serena Williams, by donating over 50 bicycles at the dedication of a newly-built park building and newly refurbished tennis courts at Leuders Park in Compton, California. An excited crowd was present to witness and celebrate this return of the sisters to their childhood home of Compton, California. It was truly wonderful to be in that moment. The two courts were officially named the Venus and Serena Williams Court of Champions and were located a few miles away from Rancho Dominguez Park where they had learned and practiced their phenomenal tennis skills years before. The Williams family would go on to establish the Yetunde Price Resource Center in Compton, to honor the life and legacy of their older sister, Yetunde Price, who lost her life in 2003 to an act of senseless violence. The center provides comprehensive services and outreach that strives to support other families in the community that suffer similar losses and all of the trauma that goes with the loss. Their philanthropy is truly endless and inspiring! I only hope that my efforts will continue to serve and support others over the course of time.

There were several other projects that I got involved with during that time. The members of the City Council of Compton were amazed at the extraordinary acts of kindness and caring going to their city by way of Alvin 'Alabama' Lovett. When they needed help with various events, they didn't hesitate to ask me for it. They started by asking me to help them with a gospel festival. I was happy to assist them. I also helped with a Thanksgiving turkey giveaway, and a Christmas parade and toy drive. The senior citizens of the community benefited when I started helping them to save for their rent. I gave more money to the schools because it's worthwhile to invest in our youth. Centennial High School, Dominguez High School, Compton Early College High School, Compton High School, and South East High School – all received my financial support.

I shared a story once at a Compton City Council Meeting. I addressed the council in a televised session to the community. During my speech, I told them something about former President Barack Obama. A gardener told me that when Obama attended Occidental College from 1979 to 1981, he made a little extra money trimming trees in Compton. The story was not officially validated, however, a mural of Barack Obama was painted on the Compton City Hall building years later. I like to believe that my story inspired someone with the idea to honor our President for helping to beautify our city. It became my mission to give to other people. It was a wonderful feeling, and highly rewarding to pass on the blessings that God bestowed upon me then, and it still is today. It would be so nice if President Obama would verify this story when he reads this book by Alvin 'Alabama' Lovett. Call him for me, if you will! I really would love to talk with you, Mr. President. I proudly supported you and worked in both your campaigns for President of these United States of America!

Blessings began to multiply and expand. I helped more schools, so they could buy basic things like uniforms to participate in intermediate sports. I supported Compton High School and Centennial High School by giving donations to sponsor their end-of-the-year athletic events. I initiated an effort to decrease gang violence and increase the idea of rivals working together. I gave financial support to the Compton Airport, which had a program that helped young people to fly across the United States, each with the help of one of the Tuskegee Airmen. I gave funds to an after-school computer drive, where students could use equipment at the airport. There was also a special program that I initiated for the City of Compton. Overall, it raised many thousands of dollars for the city and I found great joy in doing that.

After the first couple of years at Car Pros, I continued to be the top salesman. They put my name and face on a billboard along the 405 Freeway! Millions of people saw me larger than life as they drove by. I was fascinated to see my name in lights again. Coming out of a state of depression, I valued my life again. I watched The Price is Right one day and saw the oversized checks they gave away. I began to give big checks like those to the City Council for the donations to the City of Compton. I felt joy in giving away part of my income, even though my wife wasn't too thrilled. She thought that I was nutty because I was getting as much pleasure from giving, caring, and sharing as I did from receiving an income. People were bringing me more people to buy cars, which brought me a lot of awards and accolades. Let's be clear - the joy has always been in the giving. However, it does feel good to feel appreciated, and to know that you have changed people's lives for the better.

The absolute biggest winner from Alvin Alabama Lovett's hard work and image-building highlights was Car Pros Kia. 'Alabama' was most instrumental in the successes that Car Pros Kia enjoyed. The extensive community engagement and personal involvement which was the core of my successful professional life as the ultimate car salesman resulted in millions of dollars for the entire operation. Car Pros Kia became the Number One Kia dealership in the United States of America. As the Number One Salesman at Car Pros and in the country, I can proudly claim my space in the history of that company.

During the 2008/2009 recession, Car Pros Chrysler Jeep got shut down for good. The real estate business tanked, and the car business did, too. Through that process, the store was doing some things that weren't quite right. There was a lot of stress, and there were a lot of foul moves at the top. They sent the people that they wanted to keep, over to Car Pros KIA of Carson, which was down the street. They had an "adapt or quit" attitude. Leonard Fischer left the company and moved on. He didn't like the way that Car Pros was dealing with issues. He didn't want to be in that position at the KIA store.

CHAPTER 25

The Next Chapter of Visions

Remembering What Remains

For nearly a decade, I worked in community services in Mobile, Alabama. I was privileged to host 'Visions', a television show which aired on WALA-TV10 (NBC) and brought a wealth of important information and people to the citizens of Mobile. Tapes of the show covered an accumulated ten years-worth of interviews and footage that existed nowhere else. The tapes were full of stories about prominent Mobile people, locations and groundbreaking news stories. You would think that the station's archives would be full of those 'Visions' tapes, making it possible for everyone to review and re-live exciting and vital information about Mobile's history. There was an abundance of master tapes with the recorded coverage of the 'Visions' shows that were presented on TV10. My deep disappointment is that there are hardly any tapes to be found today. There are a few partial tapes on YouTube, but the great majority have been lost to the ages. No one is exactly sure how that happened.

Think about that for a minute. Being at television station WALA-TV10 (NBC) for ten years, there were significant documented historical accomplishments in the City of Mobile. The master tapes were full of stories about prominent Mobile people, locations, and important news. I had accumulated interviews and footage that showed Mobile evolving into what it is today. The following is an account of some, but definitely not all of the **'VISIONS'** shows that I recall and must pay tribute to:

Visions Television Episodes – Highlights of Community History and Legacy

Each of the following episodes of *Visions* spotlighted pivotal events, institutions, and individuals that shaped the cultural and civil rights landscape of Mobile, Alabama, and surrounding communities. For consistency, each entry below includes the episode title (or focus), a brief summary, and its historical significance.

Commonwealth National Bank (1976)

This episode chronicled the launch of Mobile's first Black-owned bank, strategically located in Toulminville to serve the predominantly African-American community. It became a pillar for financial empowerment in Mobile.

Africatown (formerly Plateau)

Visions explored the rich history of Africatown, a community founded by West Africans brought to the U.S. aboard the Clotilda—the last known illegal slave ship. The episode honored their resilience and legacy.

Dr. Martin Luther King Jr. Holiday Celebration

Covered the city's first formal observance of the MLK holiday, following efforts to establish an event itinerary. The episode captured the significance of honoring Dr. King's life and legacy locally.

Davis Avenue Renaming

Focused on the community-driven initiative to rename Jefferson Davis Avenue to Dr. Martin Luther King Jr. Avenue, reclaiming space from Confederate symbolism to honor a civil rights leader.

Saving Central High School

Documented the campaign to preserve Central High School—once a segregated institution and alma mater to many Black students—including its transition into a Bishop State Community College campus.

Franklin Primary Health Center

This episode highlighted the growth of the Franklin Health Center, founded in 1975 by Dr. Marilyn Aiello. From one location in Davis Avenue, it expanded to 23 locations across six counties, providing critical healthcare access.

HIV/AIDS Awareness in Mobile

Following the death of actor Rock Hudson, this episode promoted awareness and testing in Black communities. It featured local physicians and public education on HIV/AIDS prevention.

Lou Rawls Parade of Stars

Focused on the impact of this nationally televised UNCF fundraiser. The telethon helped support HBCUs, drawing attention to the educational needs of Black students.

The Senior Bowl

This episode covered the Senior Bowl's role in showcasing top

NFL prospects and its charitable impact in the Mobile region.

Distinguished Young Women (formerly Junior Miss Pageant)

Chronicled the Mobile-born scholarship program that empowers high school junior girls nationwide through leadership and education.

Mobile Area Mardi Gras Association (MAMGA)

Explored the founding of MAMGA in 1938 and its prominent role in Mobile's unique Mardi Gras tradition, especially through its celebrated Mammoth Parade.

The Excelsior Band

Featured Mobile's historic marching brass band, founded in 1883. It detailed their origins, impact on Mardi Gras culture, and national recognition, including a National Heritage Fellowship honor.

City Government Restructure – Wiley L. Bolden Case (1979)

Covered the legal battle to shift Mobile's government from three at-large commissioners to a mayor–council system, empowering minority representation in city politics.

Mayor Sam Jones

Celebrated the achievements of Mobile's first Black mayor (2005–2013), his prior service as County Commissioner, and the later renaming of Government Plaza in his honor.

University of South Alabama – Minority Recruitment

Focused on efforts to improve minority representation and support at the university, spotlighting advocacy and policy changes driven by community leaders.

Community Health Roundtables

Captured televised discussions with leading Black physicians addressing disparities, health access, and preventative care within Mobile.

Uplifting Prichard, Alabama

Episodes worked to counter negative stereotypes of Prichard by showcasing its residents, potential, and ongoing improvements.

Henry Aaron Loop Dedication

Documented the planning and dedication of the downtown loop named after baseball legend Hank Aaron, uniting historic streets with civil rights symbolism.

Civil Rights Leaders – Langan, LeFlore, and Montgomery

Recognized civil rights advocates Joseph Langan, John L. LeFlore, and Clarence Montgomery, including their efforts in voting rights and local activism.

Assault and Near-Lynching of Glenn Diamond (1976)

Investigated the brutality against Glenn Diamond (later Casmarah Mani), leading to national attention and advocacy at DOJ briefings.

The Lynching of Michael Donald (1981)

Examined the murder that led to a landmark civil suit against the United Klans of America, helping bankrupt the hate group through legal accountability.

Bishop State Community College

Explored the origins and growth of S. D. Bishop State, its role in educating generations of Black Alabamians, and its impact on workforce development.

Dr. Yvonne Kennedy

Profiled Dr. Kennedy's legacy as President of Bishop State, Alabama legislator, national president of Delta Sigma Theta, and guest host of *Visions*.

Voncille Thomas-Hafler

Honored her work in public education, Head Start, and community planning. She played a key role in the Foster Grandparent Program and regional development.

Douglas Wicks

Highlighted Wicks' election as Mobile's first Black County Commissioner since Reconstruction and his leadership in public housing development.

Floyd Lee King, Jr. – PUAD and the Spirit of Visions

Dedicated to the founder of People United to Advance the Dream and executive producer of *Visions*. Reflected on his mission, mentorship, and lost archival footage.

So, my television hosting experience was extensive and helped to form a core of educational showmanship that would follow me for much, if not all, of my life. There is no way that I could list all of the many episodes of 'Visions' that educated and entertained the citizens in the Channel 10 viewing area. What a privilege for me to be at the helm of a show that showcased such an indelible part of the history of Mobile and surrounding communities. All of the 'Visions' shows were timely, relevant to what was happening in Mobile, and important to the surrounding communities. The loss of those volumes of footage of important people and history-making events is not only a loss of a significant part of Mobile's history but also represents a serious disconnect from that part of everyone's past efforts to make a difference.

Despite the awful loss of so many 'Visions' episodes, the blessings of YouTube prepared a way for many to get glimpses of my televised efforts before and after my time as California's #1 Kia salesman in the nation. A quick online search will show Dr. Yvonne Kennedy speaking about her pride in the great service that I and Floyd Lee King, Jr. were doing through 'Visions' in the Greater Mobile, Alabama community.

Another search shows Car Pros Kia in Carson, California, on Black AIDS Awareness Day, supporting the Black AIDS Institute. The Honorable Congresswoman Maxine Waters was on the dais and she talked about me! Spoken at Car Pros Kia in Carson, California, on Black AIDS Awareness Day, supporting the Black AIDS Institute. Her exact words, emblazoned on my heart, were "When I walked in the door, I didn't know who Alabama was, but he came right over, introduced himself, and he has this personality. I know why he's the number one salesman! I want to thank you so very much, Alabama and CarPros Kia, for this creative and innovative way of reaching out and involving more people, and for saying to other businesses in our city, state, and country that you can do more. Let's give them a big round of applause!"

I was applauded by all of the many dignitaries in attendance, including The Honorable Mayor of Carson, California, Jim Dear. What a day! I was both lifted up and humbled to receive the amazing accolades during those times! Mayor Dear boasted, "Alabama is a key; not only can you buy a car at the right price here at the Kia dealership in Carson. Alabama is the top salesman because Alabama cares about the community. He's a man who walks his talk."

Quite wonderfully, youtube.com has provided the way for today's people and communities to see what I have been all about for much of my life. I was and continue to be 'Peculiarly Blessed' and made for such a time as this. Lord, I thank You!

CHAPTER 26

A Humble Hero

The Greatest Salesman's True Reward: Humility, Heart, and Hope

As it happened, I became more and more successful and became a top salesman in the entire nation over the next few years. Receiving recognition as the top Kia salesman from all LA car salesmen all over the United States of America is an honor. Coming from Mobile AL and making it in the huge LA market is an astonishing feat. I even surprised myself. Humility and focus continue to be my keys to helping people in need. I give my help to everyone. However, taking care of my people is a priority. I work hard to help the poverty-stricken, and other areas of the black community. If we don't help our own, who will? I give a hand out to anybody in need. At Car Pros Kia, I became a better salesman and grew as a person.

Car Pros Kia gave me a department with people who worked directly under me. Six of my people came from the community. They distributed flyers introducing me to the community and describing all of the benefits available, when doing business with Alvin 'Alabama' Lovett of Car Pros Kia. From ten to fifteen thousand flyers were distributed each month all over LA. Headed by Randy Anderson, they also worked the 'Taste of Soul' event, The MLK Parade that drew over a million people, the Gay Pride Parade, and every church in LA. That group was paid from the same source as the one responsible for printing the flyers – Alvin 'Alabama' Lovett.

My liaison with the churches who reached out and contacted officers and members of the churches was Ann Wiley from Selma, Alabama. We assisted pastors, officers and members who were in need of transportation to get financial help so they could purchase new and used vehicles. All over LA, during that time, pastors preached about Alvin 'Alabama' Lovett. From the churches' pulpit to the gospel radio waves, including KJLH which was owned by Stevie Wonder, the message was the same. Everyone was welcome at Car Pros Kia. Mailers went out to the churches on a regular basis that explained Alvin 'Alabama' Lovett's heart for serving the poor, pastors and church members of the African American community. People came to know that 'Alabama' would sponsor several large and small churches on the radio out of his own pocket, at different times.

The Car Pros Kia dealership provided 'Alabama' with a full-time secretary to run his desk. They also provided a delivery person in finishing with the car delivery, at times when another salesman would help deliver the purchase. Whenever another salesman helped manage the very large daily turnout of customers who came looking for 'Alabama' neither Kia Corporate or Car Pros Kia would give me any credit for those purchases. With the high volume of customers that I bought into the dealership daily, I was lucky to be credited with three out of ten sales generated by me. I felt that this was sad and unfair treatment.

Because of the large number of 'Alabama' generated customers coming into the dealership, new departments were created to sell to "Alabama's" customers, with no effort made to ensure that I would be compensated or credited with those sales. The same held true for the personal funds that I used to generate the increased traffic and sales revenue linked to 'Alabama'. A department in-service was set up that informed all staff that re-sales or upgrades for "Alabama's" previously sold customers would be handled by newly hired sales-people. Internet and new hires sales people were given a list that included 'Alabama' customers and were told to outreach by telephone, for other sales people. Walk-in customers who asked for 'Alabama' were told that I was with other customers and that they would help since I was "so busy". Truth or not, I still did not receive any credit for the flourishing business. Not one person in the dealership was redirected, reprimanded or punished for selling cars this way. I later found out that other dealerships did not treat their top salesmen as I was treated.

The biggest day of my car-selling career was when actress Vanessa Williams came into the dealership.The Vanessa Williams who played Keisha in *New Jack City* (1991). Ms. Williams was representing the Black Aids Institute and was accompanied by radio personality Tammie Mack, from Stevie Wonder's SLH radio station. They had come to the 'Kia Forte Raffle', an event that I had created and worked on for a full year. For this event, customers who would take an HIV/AIDS test would win one chance to win a car. After I had spent thousands of my own dollars and countless work hours in the community promoting this event, car buyers flocked to the lot. At that time, management asked me to allow other sales people to work with my customers. I agreed to cooperate and 72 cars were sold on this one day! This was the biggest one-day accomplishment of my career in car sales – 72 CARS! Unfortunately, I was credited and paid for only three (3) of those cars, after creating 72 total sales. I hope this explains just how the 'Greatest Salesman in the United States' (my self-titled moniker) was treated. It's quite possible that I was impacting and saving thousands of lives in the LA community. HIV/AIDS was present and wreaking havoc in the African-American community in LA and around the country. Testing was so very critical to stem the tide of the horrific sickness and death which AIDS brought to LA citizens. The most important thing was that this event was a success for both Car Pros Kia and the community. As for myself, even though I did not reap fame or fortune that day, we must know and accept that God has His Own Purpose in our lives. It is not always my will but His Will be done. I trust Him. I am His humble servant.

When I came to Leonard all of those years ago, I didn't look ready to work. However, when I had a chance, I took steps to make things better. If the people in charge had their way, they would not have hired me, but there was no denying me. You can't take away a man's hard work. Leonard helped me as much as he could while he was around. He once said, "Alabama is his own genius and has his own vision." I am extremely grateful to have seen my vision come to life.

There were many challenges, but I found a way to live my life. I used my work ethic, made a greater platform for myself inside the job, and accomplished great things for the community. There was a time when I thought I was just a few car sales behind the top guy in the country. Leonard said that I was actually "light years ahead." To this day, we have an unbroken bond, and I always treat him like family.

Leonard believed that I could do even bigger things because I don't give up. Other than my wife, he was the only one who believed in me back then. His faith began on day one and has never wavered. Destiny brought us together. We were both blessed to have met each other that day. We were on different paths but were brought together in the right place at the right time. The story of my friendship with Leonard Fischer is a lesson in giving people a chance. You can't look at someone and know his or her worth. Leonard is doing well for himself these days. He feels blessed to be my good friend, and I feel equally honored to be his. Leonard Fischer is one of my heroes.

I am still amazed and grateful at the way in which God ordered my steps in this world. Being from LA (that's Lower Alabama y'all) and ending up in Los Angeles put me on a path where my wife Joyce and I would visit and enjoy many different parts of the world. Bona fide disasters were also blessings. It's safe to say that in 2005 Hurricane Katrina was a disaster for a lot of people, but it was a blessing for me. I had gone back to my hometown of Mobile to help others, and then God stepped in. Going back there took me away from the alcohol that I was immersed in. Some have said that I was self-medicating so I could manage my symptoms of PTSD. Post-Traumatic Stress Disorder (PTSD) had taken me as a hostage in my own life story. This came about after the shoot-out at the LA Times newspaper. That shoot-out terrified me! Not only did I lose control of my bodily functions, I was left with a lack of will-power to do anything productive with my life. I drank more than any other time in my life. I was left with a mindset of unproductive energy where I only focused on life's losers and figuring out why people give up! If I had not gone to help the Katrina victims in Mobile, I would still be doing wrong. Life for me would have remained unchallenging and unproductive. I would have gone from Lower Alabama to Los Angeles and, most important of all, I would not have passed that breathalyzer test and become Alvin 'Alabama' Lovett, car salesman extraordinaire! I had kept company with and listened to many homeless people tell their story of failure, loss and disappointment, why people go to prison, drugs, crimes, mental decay, financial ruin, divorce, murder, suicide, prostitution, violence, confusion, gambling, delusions, psychosis, being an introvert, meanness, and anger. Even though I was most likely in the same swirling toilet as my comrades, it reminded me that God always has a plan. Sometimes He leads you down a short path. Then there is another path with all of the ups, downs, twists, and turns of a roller-coaster. The important thing is to see every detail along the way and to know that wherever you end up, it will be a blessing. Hurricane Katrina allowed me to be a blessing to others. It ultimately saved my sanity.

At this juncture, President George W. Bush had become a very unpopular president. There was the rise of a new gentleman by the name of Barack Obama, who became the 44th President of the United States in 2009. When President Obama got into office, he set up a program called the Car Allowance Rebate System (CARS), also known as Cash for Clunkers. All manufacturers of cars in America restructured their finances, and Chrysler applied to the government for help. President Obama required the manufacturers to have fuel efficient cars. That's how they could receive funding. The deal did not go through. Chrysler only had their gas guzzlers, even though the cars were still in high demand in America. Eventually, Chrysler had to downsize. There was a raffle to see what division would stay in Los Angeles, and our dealership closed. Ken Phillips Car Pros Chrysler Jeep went away and they kept Kia. I made a decision about my new career, and stayed with Ken Phillips. Car Pros Kia moved down the block on Avalon in 2009. I went with them, and we sold cars under the Cash for Clunkers program. Kia had models named Spectra and Rio, which were both fuel-efficient. We sold them like IHOP sold pancakes.

Ken Phillips was the best in the business. He was supportive of me, and just as I was the top salesman at Car Pros Chrysler Jeep, I became the top salesman at Car Pros Kia. Community involvement became greater for me as I continued working on the Martin Luther King Day Holiday. I also expanded what I was doing for students all over Los Angeles, Compton, Gardena, Paramount, Carson, Long Beach, and San Pedro. I continued to help and give. Eventually, I spent over $2000.00 per month of my own money to purchase materials and make donations to schools. Most spouses would not accept that much to be taken out of the budget. I thank my wife for dealing with my insanity or compassion or both. I thank Joyce for allowing me to give away whatever I had so that I could help people. During my career, I spent over $250,000 of my own money to promote Car Pros Kia into becoming the nation's top dealership.

Car Pros Kia was flourishing. The business grew as more and more people came in asking for 'Alabama'. The other salesmen must have been jealous. They were always tricking people into buying from them, and I would not get credit, even though they were using my name. However, that could not deter me. I was doing God's work, and because of my significant efforts, the word got out that Car Pros was a caring business, always giving back to the community.

Years later, Car Pros Kia and I got together with Phill Wilson and the Black AIDS Institute. Phill was President and Chief Executive Officer. He is also my wife's cousin. Phill is a man of great courage, wisdom and foresight. Since there is no possible way to do a brief summary of his accolades, please take the time to read the following, from their website:

Prior to founding the Institute, Wilson served as the AIDS Coordinator for the City of Los Angeles from 1990 to 1993, the Director of Policy and Planning at AIDS Project Los Angeles from 1993 to 1996. He was co-chair of the Los Angeles County HIV Health Commission from 1990 to 1995, and was an appointee to the HRSA AIDS Advisory Committee from 1995 to 1998. Wilson was the coordinator of the International Community Treatment and Science Workshop at the 12th, 13th, 14th, 15th, and 16th International AIDS Conferences in Geneva, Switzerland; Durban, South Africa; Barcelona, Spain; Bangkok, Thailand; and Toronto, Canada.

Wilson was the co-founder of the National Black Lesbian and Gay Leadership Forum and the National Task Force on AIDS Prevention. He has been involved in the founding of a number of other AIDS service organizations and community-based organizations, including the Chris Brownlie Hospice-AIDS Healthcare Foundation, the National Minority AIDS Council, the Los Angeles County Gay Men of Color Consortium, and the CAEAR Coalition.

The Ford Foundation named Wilson one of the 20 award recipients for the Leadership for a Changing World, in 2001. He was a member of the U.S. delegation to the 1994 World AIDS Summit in Paris, and has worked extensively on HIV/AIDS policy, research, prevention, and treatment issues in Russia, Latvia, the Ukraine, the UK, Holland, Germany, France, Mexico, South Africa, Zimbabwe, Zambia, Tanzania, India, and Botswana. He has published articles in the Los Angeles Times, New York Times, LA Weekly, Essence, Ebony, Vibe, Jet, POZ, HIV+ and other periodicals.

Wilson is a recent recipient of the Delta Spirit Award from the Delta Sigma Theta Los Angeles chapter. He was given the Discovery Health Channel Medical Honor in July 2004 and was recently named one of the "2005 Black History Makers in the Making" by Black Entertainment Television. Wilson holds a BA in

Fine Arts from Illinois Wesleyan University. He currently resides in Los Angeles, California.

This was a major collaboration. We made an agreement which would allow people to come to the dealership to get tested for HIV/AIDS, and we would enter their names in a raffle to win a free car. We did that for four years and gave away four cars. The dealership received global recognition, which enhanced its image. Even Hollywood became involved, and we got Congressional recommendations from the highest levels of our government. All of the cities in the surrounding areas of Southern California gave recognition to Car Pros, who helped the Black Aids Institute, under the leadership of Wilson, to achieve the best numbers in testing that they had reached in years. Many of the largest cities in the country had offices. An HIV/AIDS testing van, with my picture on it, went all over Southern California and covered almost all of the colleges and universities. The testing van appeared in the Martin Luther King Day, Christmas, and Gay and Lesbian Pride parades, reaching more people than ever imagined. The 'Alabama' name, along with the Black Aids Institute and Car Pros Kia, became a household brand of recognition to millions of people, creating tremendous revenue to help spiral the Car Pros Kia dealership, and the fast-growing Kia Company into becoming number one in the world.

Photo Courtesy of Alvin 'Alabama' Lovett

The Black Aids Institute has a multitude of celebrities, politicians, business people and ordinary people doing extraordinary things in support of their cause. Each year they honor Heroes in the Struggle. High profile people who have been honored and/or supportive of Phill Wilson and the organization, are Dionne Warwick, an activist and pioneer in the struggle, Cookie Johnson, wife of Magic Johnson, Tony Award-winner Billy Porter, talk show and radio show host Tavis Smiley, actors Gloria Reuben, Danny Glover, and Sheryl Lee Ralph, politicians Diane Watson and Jesse Jackson, and Sandra Evers-Manley, founder of the Black

Hollywood Education and Resource Center. Countless others have supported the Black Aids Institute. I am so proud to be among the list of people who go above and beyond to help save lives.

I want to give special thanks to Ken Phillips, the owner of Car Pros Kia, who allowed me to give away cars to the Black Aids Institute, and for all of the many ways in which he facilitated my dreams and wishes. The marketing of Car Pros Kia became well pronounced on local television, on radio, and through social media. The company was highly advocated by many churches throughout the Los Angeles area, urging people to go to Car Pros Kia and buy their cars from 'Alabama'. Newspapers and social organizations, who did other types of charitable work, involved me in their promotions. There were many ways in which I was utilized, and given a platform to touch even more lives in the Southern California communities through my work of giving back.

Car Pros Kia sales grew, and a new building was erected a mile away, creating the largest Kia dealership in the United States. I was not the only source of Kia customers, but I was significantly involved in the company's growth. Pro athletes like Blake Griffin, formerly of the Los Angeles Clippers, and other basketball players, endorsed the name 'Alabama'. Jamal Crawford, also of the LA Clippers, donated cars to The Boys Club, with the help of Alvin 'Alabama' Lovett. Hollywood stars, elected officials, and organizations throughout the city supported my causes. There were even managers at other Kia dealerships who recognized such benefits from my name that they assigned an 'Alabama' salesman to attract more business to their dealerships. Interestingly enough, those dealers who allowed their sales people to be called 'Alabama' when car buyers called or came in to buy cars were not necessarily black, but white, Asian, Mexican, Middle Eastern, or even African! Of course, I didn't get compensated for any of that. With all of the money made from the 'Alabama' name, folks might expect me to be living large. They would be wrong. Although I had a happy home with Joyce, we still lived in a modest mobile home in Compton, all while I'm making millions of dollars for others.

I can trace the success all the way back to my ventures off the lot, which the dealership thought was crazy, but launched the flood of customers who came in and asked for 'Alabama'. And then there was the multitude of customers who came in from the 'hood with my flyers. The other salesmen would not have come up with those ideas in a million years. I assume most of them didn't even know their way to the 'hood'. Despite all of that, I continued to be a real team player, even playing a significant role in the sale of Kia from Ken Phillips to the Trophy Group, who now runs the large Carson lot and the Kia dealership of Los Angeles Downtown.

CHAPTER 27

Alabama Buttermilk

The Making of a Humble Hero

Each and every day of my life, I try to represent Mobile well and do my part to make things better. Mobile will always be near and dear to me. I'm a man with a plan—someone who moves with purpose and knows when the time is right to act. When I came to Compton, I embraced it fully. No matter how much money I make, I'm not chasing after what others might consider a "better" city or situation. I love being in Compton. I love being in a community where I can make a meaningful difference. If I ever move again, it will be to return to where it all began—Mobile, Alabama.

On July 2, 2017, the city of Mobile honored me with a day of recognition for my contributions as a citizen and for my work in television and radio journalism that helped bring about positive change. That moment meant the world to me. Joyce and I are doing well. We cherish our families and stay as connected as we can. Both of my brothers, Britt and LaGrand, have passed on, each leaving behind a child—Britt had a son and a daughter, and LaGrand had a daughter. Life brought its challenges, and for a time, we found ourselves away from the church.

Eventually, we found our way back into our spiritual rhythm. We joined Second Baptist Church under the leadership of Pastor William Epps, and it felt like home. We've been there ever since, grounded in our faith and grateful for the journey.

I lost track of my old friend Arthur Mack after he joined the Navy in 1977. Decades passed before we reconnected on Facebook in 2011. By then, a lot had changed in both of our lives. Arthur had heard whispers about my involvement in AA and the struggles I had faced—failed marriages, business setbacks, and other personal challenges. But he never fed into the negativity. Arthur dealt in facts and kept a clear head. He believed some of the rumors were rooted in jealousy and chose not to repeat what he couldn't verify. That kind of loyalty meant a lot to me. After all, I had once been a role model to him.

As we rekindled our friendship online, I found joy in cheering him on. When the University of South Alabama published its 50th-anniversary book, Arthur was featured for his many accomplishments since graduation. I read his profile with pride and made sure to let him know how happy I was to see all that he had achieved.

There were moments when I didn't know where to turn or who to trust—but I always felt God's hand guiding me. I've come to understand that divine help doesn't always arrive in the form we expect. Sometimes it's a kind word from a stranger, a timely phone call, or a door that opens just when you feel trapped. Angels don't always have wings—they might wear work boots or carry grocery bags.

Over the years, I learned that even imperfect people can be used for a perfect purpose. Some of the individuals God placed in my life were deeply flawed, just like I was. But they served a role—lifting me up when I couldn't stand on my own. Every time I thought I was drowning, He sent something to keep me afloat. It may not have looked like a life raft, but it was enough. There's no mountain too high or valley too deep for His grace to reach. Trusting that truth has carried me further than I ever imagined.

I believe that's what sets me apart in the eyes of some people. We may all come from the same place, poured into the same bucket of life experiences. But just like buttermilk naturally rises and separates, some of us are called to become something distinct—something that adds richness, depth, and value to everything around it. That's what *Alabama Buttermilk* represents to me: standing out not for attention, but for purpose, refinement, and contribution.

THE END

ACKNOWLEDGMENTS

"Al is a prime example of somebody having it all, and then losing it all and regaining it again. If anybody wants to look at Exhibit A of somebody who has fallen on hard times, but battled back to become somebody special, someone who is positive, and doing positive things for the community, they can look at Al Lovett. That would be Exhibit A, in my opinion."
Arthur L. Mack

"Al Lovett represents Mobile, Alabama well and wants to make things happen. Mobile is near and dear to him. He came to Compton, and no matter how much money he makes, he's not trying to move into a better city or a better situation. He loves being in Compton, being in the community to do something special, and if he ever leaves, it will only be to go back to where he began, Mobile, Alabama."
Leonard Fischer

I first met Alabama when we were both working as salesmen at Car Pros Kia. We competed against each other to become the top salesman, striving to make Car Pros Kia the number one dealership in America. Many years later, I returned to Kia of Carson and became Alabama's manager. Despite the passage of time, Alabama maintained the same competitive drive he had when we first sold cars together at the original Car Pros Kia.

When I managed Alabama, he often had more customers than he could personally assist. There were times when five to ten customers would request him at once, and other salesmen would help with these customers, but Alabama would not receive credit for those sales. Unlike some dealerships where an owner-partner could receive credit for sales made by others, Alabama only got credit for the cars he actually delivered. This meant he might be responsible for ten customers but only receive credit for three. Therefore, the recognition of Alabama's greatness as a salesman might not fully reflect his true achievements, as his numbers were far greater than the corporate office would ever know.

The beauty of Alabama's work ethic was that he exerted just as much, if not more, effort to help customers with credit challenges as he did for those with excellent credit. In an industry driven by the motivation to make money, no smart salesman would typically prioritize customers who might not yield immediate compensation. I often directed Alabama to focus on customers with good credit to ensure he got paid, but I would later find him helping those with less credit, earning less money for those sales. Sometimes, it seemed Alabama treated the dealership like a church rather than a business, choosing to help those in need.

As a top salesman, Alabama traveled the world on reward trips from Kia. His office walls were adorned with plaques and certificates from every city government in our area, including Los Angeles, Inglewood, Gardena, Compton, Long Beach, and acknowledgments from the United States Congress and the California Governor's Office. Alabama was recognized by movie stars, churches, and community organizations throughout Southern California. He even missed a free throw at a Los Angeles Clippers game that could have earned him around $50,000.

Alabama worked with basketball players like slam dunk champion Blake Griffin to donate automobiles and collaborated with Aaron Jamal Crawford of the All-Star Los Angeles Clippers to donate a car to the Boys Club in Compton, California. He represented the dealership in gifting fifty bicycles when the city of Compton recognized Venus and Serena Williams. Alabama was deeply involved in HIV/AIDS awareness, donating several automobiles to the Black AIDS Institute to promote testing in African American neighborhoods and colleges throughout Southern California cities.

Alabama's face was displayed on the billboard facing the 405 Freeway, the busiest traffic corridor in Southern California. He appeared in the Martin Luther King Jr. Day Parade, which is the largest event promoting Kia in the United States. Alabama frequently sponsored donations of books and school supplies to Southern California schools. I was told that Alabama was responsible for selling 73 cars in one day while working with KJLH, a radio station owned by Stevie Wonder, with Tammi Mac KJLH DJ. They also raffled off a brand-new car with actress Vanessa Williams to promote HIV/AIDS testing.

Alabama collaborated with the Black AIDS Institute and Car Pros Kia in a significant effort that involved prominent figures such as movie director Lee Daniels, actors Alfre Woodard, Cheryl Lee Ralph, Danny Glover, and Taraji P. Henson, as well as Gina Belafonte, the daughter of Harry Belafonte. This initiative also saw the participation of Magic and Cookie Johnson at Jamie Foxx's estate. Many of the events recognizing heroes in the fight against HIV/AIDS were held at the Screen Actors Guild in Los Angeles, California.

It is remarkable how this type of community effort raised awareness among car buyers that Car Pros Kia cared about the community. These efforts contributed to a single month in which Car Pros Kia was able to sell nine hundred cars.

Before my arrival, I learned that Alabama had donated a van to a homeless shelter in Watts that provided housing for women and children. I personally witnessed Alabama spending a significant amount of money out of his own pocket to distribute ads, literature, and flyers throughout California, encouraging people to ask for him at the Kia dealership. I was honored to work as his manager during the time leading up to COVID-19. Many people would say that Alabama was more than just a salesman; he was a spokesperson for the Kia corporation. Now retired and having moved back to Alabama, I wish him well in his retirement with his wife, Joyce. There is no car salesman in Southern California who hasn't heard of Alvin "Alabama" Lovett.
Hassan Chahine – 'Alabama's Manager at Kia Of Carson

'Alabama' is truly one of the greatest people I've ever met in my life. To me, he is a celebrity. He's gracious, witty, intelligent, giving, and an incredible soul. He goes out of his way to help people and is an absolute sweetheart. I have witnessed his charity in many ways. There were times that he employed people who were literally homeless. He was budgeting from his own salary to advertise, and would find folks on the street to give them jobs passing out flyers. 'Alabama' is very tactful and caring with his customers. He is articulate and resourceful in a legitimate way.

When I first met him, I was working at the Huntington Beach store prior to me becoming his manager at the Carson store. When he came in, he walked up and handed me his card. He said his name was 'Alabama' and I should call him if I ever needed a car. It was such a pleasure working with him. His motivation, his drive for life, his passion for humanity. Everything about him, I truly love. He's just amazing. I invited him to my 50th birthday party at my house and my entire family, including my in-laws, fell in love with him. They were infatuated by him. He's such a character and so charismatic. I wish that there were more people in the world like him.

I quit Car Pros Kia in February of 2017, so I was not there during the time that the store was sold by Ken Phillips, however, enough things happened during my time that showed me that 'Alabama' was compromised. For what he has accomplished, and all that he has done for the black community, he should have been given so much more from the company. And what he did with the Black AIDS Institute was amazing. He introduced well-known actors, singers and other celebrities, bringing them together in a cohesive unit to fight HIV/AIDS. By bringing the Car Pros name into the equation, he was able to raffle off cars for needy families and be a contributor for the Black Aids Institute. He did things to help get people off the street and cleaned up. He sponsored kids to go on educational trips and have opportunities. I can go on and on.

'Alabama' was overlooked by the owners and management of Car Pros. They tried many different ways to accommodate him, but those processes were wrong to begin with, and the implementation of those processes was even worse. They gave him his own department, but undermined him and his intelligence by giving him the pits, basically. For such a huge, lucrative business to do that was really a shame. After all of the years that 'Alabama' planted the seeds and had a portfolio of customers who religiously asked for him, they would pass the customers off to other salesmen, totally bypassing ‘Alabama’. It was disgraceful. I witnessed it time in and time out. The only reason they came to Car Pros was to see ‘Alabama’. If he was busy or not there, salesmen would steal his customers, without him knowing or getting his due compensation. The management knew about it and just let it happen. It was unjust and got worse and worse.

By the end of my term, I tried to talk to ‘Alabama’ and ease his pain. If he had a chance to sell a car to everyone who came in to ask for him, he would be selling at least 75 to 100 cars a month. When it came time to sell the place, the former owners should have expressed to the new owners how important an asset they were getting with ‘Alabama’. He was a gem, and should have been protected. He was loyal for all those years and he was treated really, really poorly. Everything that he did created advertising for the company, as well as for himself, but his motivation has always been selfless. Part of “Alabama’s” demise was in his loyalty to Ken Phillips. With his track record and popularity, he could have gotten a job anywhere, and his thousands of customers would have followed him. But that loyalty was not reciprocated.

Even though I was his boss, he inspired and motivated me in the way that he treated people with dignity, contributed to humanity, and contributed to his business. He treated people with respect, the way that he wanted to be treated, regardless of their credit score, regardless of their status in life, or their current situation. Even when he couldn’t make the deal, he encouraged them to come back after they saved their money. God Bless him with many, many years of good and healthy life.
David Panah

My daughter and I met Alabama about 3 years ago at Kia of Cerritos and it was only God that brought us together! The car I had, at the time, was having a major issue which I already knew was going to end up emptying my pockets!

While my daughter and I were sitting in the waiting area to hear what the damage was going to be, there came an Angel in disguise coming to greet us named "Alabama". He inquired as to why I was there and I explained the situation about my car. He said, "how about a new car?" I said, "I can't afford a new car right now", and he said something like, "you never know what Blessings God has in store for you", I said, "you're absolutely right". He then said, "well let's go pick out your new car" and outside we went. I finally picked out the car I liked and to make a long story a bit shorter, Alabama helped me to get into that brand new car, with very little down, all while I was still waiting to hear what it was going to cost to fix my car!

Before they could even tell me the cost to fix my car, Alabama had let them know I was getting a new car! As I was finalizing paperwork, they finally called me to the service area and told me the cost to fix my car. The cost was way more than what I needed for the down payment on my new car. I decided out with the old and in with the new and off into the sunset my daughter and I went in our new car! What a Blessing that was.

I thank God for placing Alabama at that Kia of Cerritos at that exact time to help me! My daughter and I will never forget that moment and never forget our Angel, Alabama!

Alvin "Alabama" Lovett is a Blessing and a wonderful Gift from God to humanity!

Peace, Love and Many Blessings Always.
Daphne & Christina Spell

I first experienced the pleasure of meeting Mr. Alvin "Alabama" Lovett back on June 1 of 2011 at Car Pros Kia. I had heard about him through friends in the car business as the "Man who Sells the most Kia Cars in the USA." This man was a giant legend in the industry. I had been hired into the service department to help increase service sales and customer CSI.

I was introduced to Alabama by the service director and then realized that he was truly a "giant in the industry". Standing at almost 7" tall and larger than life, he quickly made an impression on me. His smile was genuine and his demeanor was that of professional calm but confidence in that he would genuinely sell you a car.

After a week I built a relationship with him where I wanted to refer customers and friends to him, who were in need of a car, but more than that, a person who actually cared about his clients. Alabama is also very spiritual and just one of those persons who gives back to his community and never is looking for a hand-out. Pretty soon I was sending him a ton of prospective clients. He always came back to me and thanked me personally and expressed his gratitude, which was something that most sales people just didn't do!!

I left Car Pros later on and remained friends with Alabama after I opened 3 of my own independent dealerships. People that he could not get financed, he referred them to me. I offered to pay him a referral fee, but he declined. Instead, he asked that I donate it to a worthy cause.

I struck up an affiliation with Temple Hills Baptist Church and pastor Torey. We immediately started a faith-based leasing program for all of his congregation and those within Pastor Torey's other religious affiliations. I also donated a 14-passenger van for the Martin Luther King Day parade and over $20,000 to start a youth training program for after school projects, in order to pay my community forward. We donated food and a car to the community of East Los Angeles through the local Catholic Church.

All of this was inspired by my good friend Alabama!!! When my friend Michael lost his wife suddenly, Alabama was there to rescue his soul!! I thought that Michael would do something desperate and Alabama's calming and caring voice got Michael grounded and back with God!! I cannot say enough great things that this Great Man has inspired me to be. I can tell you that I am in awe for the things that he continues to do!!! I am also in awe about the things he accomplished from his past!!! God Bless Alabama and his Family!
Walter Simmons

I have known 'Alabama' for many years. Met him at Car Pros Kia in 2012. We worked together until November, 2017, when I left to go to another Kia dealership. He would come visit me and we continued keeping in touch. Great guy, really hard worker. He's one of the best at what he does. He has always taken money out of his own pocket to bring clientele to the dealership. He was spending an average of $2,000.00 a month for all of the years that I've known him. He did a lot for his customers, giving them gifts, giving them money. Anything he could do to help the community. He didn't really care about the money. All of this came from his personal finances. He's one of a kind. He has a huge heart. If you're struggling, he will be there for you one hundred percent. He really helped Car Pros Kia to be what it is right now and when they sold the company, they didn't take him into consideration. After he built the clientele for them, and used his own resources to make it happen, they just left him out. I don't think that was cool. The owner didn't even give him a chance to go with them. They abandoned him after all that he did, and after using him. And they used him a whole lot. He was selling an average of forty plus cars a month, and sometimes fifty. That doesn't include the ones that they would steal from him. The reality is that his clients bought about eighty cars a month, but he would only get credit for half, because they were stealing from him. The other thing is that 'Alabama' would do rallies and go to churches, anything he could do to bring more business to Car Pros Kia.

He would pay employees under him to do follow-ups and pass out mailers. He would never stop. There's something that we did together. 'Alabama' was always making it to platinum sales, which means he was a top salesman in the country. Once, he was a little short. He needed to sell 72 cars in twenty days. He went around asking everybody for help and nobody wanted to help him. Nobody believed in him because 72 cars, in 20 days, was unheard of, and nobody would help. They said it couldn't be done. He even went to the General Manager and the General Sales Manager, which was David Panah. They laughed at him and assured him that he wouldn't be going on the trip that year. When he came to me for help, I was the only one who said I would help him. I said 'Don't worry, 'Alabama'. You will be on that trip". I went to work those twenty days with 'Alabama', from 9am to 10pm, never taking a day off. We did the 70 plus cars and no one could believe that we did it. He even got really sick on the last three days. I told him to sit in the showroom and say hello to the customers and I did everything else. He went to the annual trip.

When I first got to the dealership, they showed me the reports and I knew that 'Alabama' was the number one guy there. We became very good friends. All of the cars that I sold for him, I put in his name. I didn't charge him anything. Basically, I worked for free. As a result of the sales, he won a L60" Plasma TV. He told me to bring my car around and put it in my trunk. It was a gift from him to me. Nobody could believe me.
Narciso Alvarez

My late husband Gerard Burton and I met Alvin Alabama Lovett, in 2011 face to face, but technically we'd known of him a little longer. My Mother in love the late Mary Burton had first gotten her car. We knew exactly who we wanted to help us at Kia Of Carson. Alabama made us feel comfortable immediately. I told him we had a trade-in and that I wanted a truck, oh, and let me not forget to mention our credit wasn't too hot. After working through the kinks Alabama told us we were approved for a used truck. He told us to pay our note on time for at least 13 months so that he could get us in a truck. Sure enough, we did our part and less than a year we were in our new truck.

My husband and I have gotten many vehicles from Alabama as well as my family. From 2009 until, I believe, 2022 my family has gotten between 15 to 20 cars from Alabama. One last thing I have a Podcast 'Heart Of Worship w/Dani B JAIA'. I'm proud to say Alvin Alabama Lovett was my special guest. His story

captivated my audience and to this day is still a favorite. That day I learned more about how Alabama is so infectious and loved by all who come into contact with him.
Danielle Burton

My name is Ms. Sonya Adams, Founder/President of the 7-time award winning nonprofit charity organization, Celebrating A Vision. We provide amazing experiences to cancer survivors & foster kids. All at no cost! Most of what we do is out of pocket so it's important for us to have sponsorships. I reached out to 'Alabama', and he answered the call. We were able to have a fundraiser and raise money for some of our upcoming projects. 'Alabama' also personally donated. His commitment and dedication to the community is Priceless. His strong faith in God has shaped him into the man we all come to know and love. His work ethic is top tier and is at a level you just don't see today.

He has great customer service skills and his approach to selling cars is warm and inviting. You don't ever feel stressed or pressured. His track record is unmatched and speaks for itself. Winning top selling sales man year after year. We are grateful to have crossed paths with a man with so much wisdom & rich history.
Sonya Adams

I met Alabama about 10 years ago. I was a white bill collector who went to his Kia Dealership to collect. I also had the crazy idea that I could persuade Alabama to get an ad in a new publication I was starting. Alabama knew everyone. He knew politicians and sold cars to many of them. I was a nobody, my publication was little more than a dream, but Alabama decided to give this bill collector a try. In the beginning he paid for the advertisements out of his own pocket. Later Kia corporate picked up the bill. I wasn't the only person he helped. He & his dealership did benefits for aids research and gave Kias away to promote education. Even though he and his wife have moved back to Alabama, he stays in touch and thinks of ways to help this former bill collector out.

Richard Vaughn

A glimpse of our neighborhood during the 60's and 70's. First, I was born at 413 1/2 N Franklin Street at the corner of Beauregard and Franklin Streets in 1953. I was the fourth child born to Dan and Lillian McCord. I had one older brother, Dan Jr, and two sisters, Loretta and Linda. About 1957, we moved several blocks South and three blocks East to 354 N Jackson Street. The neighborhood was a mixture of black and white. As the whites moved out, some of the most amazing black families moved in. As the neighborhood continued to grow, all the children and families became as one big family that spanned about four blocks in each direction. If you dared to go in any direction, there was always a parent to keep you straight. I can name most of those families still today. In the next block from 354 N Jackson Street, on the corner of Jackson and Adams Street, there was Willie Mae's Cafe. A few doors West of Willie Mae's Cafe was where the Lovett family lived, a beautiful brick home as most were wood framed homes. There were two brothers, LaGrand and Alvin Lovett. LaGrand and my brother, Dan Jr, were good friends, Alvin, a few years younger than LaGrand, seemed to be into books and business. When you saw Alvin, he was always dressed and would occasionally wear a necktie. My brother wouldn't let me hang out with them because I was too young.

On Jackson Street and Adams Street, several doors down was the Tunstall Hotel, one of only two hotels in Mobile where black travelers could stay. I hated the Tunstall Hotel because we the boys in the neighborhood would play football in the streets with an orange juice carton packed with sand. There were days when we wanted to play football in the street, but we couldn't because on different occasions, buses would be parked in the street in front of our house and Ms. Louise. The buses would have on them, James Brown and the Fabulous Flames / The Motown Review / Poo-Nanny's Review and others like Howling Wolf, Gorgeous George, Rufus Thomas, Traveling Black Baseball Teams and many more.

On Adams Street, at the corner of Jackson Street, on the corner across from the Lovett's, lived a heavy-set lady name Ms. Elouise and her husband who was a seaman. Because of his height, everyone called him 'Long'. When the Tunstall Hotel was full, Ms. Elouise would rent rooms out to them. At my age, about 10 years old, we didn't care who they were, all we knew was that we wanted them and their buses gone and out of the way so we could play in the street. There was a time when James Brown was doing a show in Mobile and their buses were parked where we played. James Brown's backup singers would be practicing their dance steps and we could hear some of the band members playing their instruments. My friends and myself called them "sissies" because they wore their hair "processed" and scarfs tied around their heads. The buses were never there more than two days. Blues singer Howling Wolf would stay at the Tunstall Hotel and would sometimes stay longer than a week. He would be sitting on a wooden bench outside of Willie Mae's Cafe talking to the longshoremen workers as if he worked at the Alabama State Docks. He would usually be dressed in overhauls and a shirt with a cigar in his hand or mouth. On a couple of occasions, he told me, "boy, run round there to that store and get me three White Owl cigars. He would give me a half dollar piece and told me to keep the change. White Owl cigars were ten cents apiece and twenty cents was good pocket change. You could buy a lot with twenty cents.

There were other entertainers who stayed at the Tunstall Hotel. I once saw a bus with the Motown Review on it, but I never saw any of them because the bus was parked already when I went outside to play. I remember Sam Cook and Otis Redding, a group called Poo-Nanny's Review and others who were either at I.L.A. 1410 Union Hall or Ed Tucker's Club and the Harlem Duke in Prichard.

Around the corner from the Lovett family, on Congress Street between Claiborne and Franklin Streets lived an older lady who was bedridden and she had two sons or grandsons, they were Aaron and Zack. One went to sea and the other went astray.

I had grown to be about 15 years of age, and I delivered groceries by way of a big bicycle with a basket on the front of it. That's when I was at a seafood market on Claiborne Street and I was in there talking to Johnnie Mae Brookings when three well-dressed men came in. They looked familiar but I couldn't grasp who they were until Johnnie Mae screamed "MELVIN!' and in a heavy voice he said "Hey Johnnie Mae". Then she said "Sam, these are the Temptations".

It was Melvin English Franklin, Eddie Kendricks and Dennis Edwards. Eddie Kendricks bought about four packs of cigarettes and they bought other things. They were doing a show at the Municipal Auditorium and Melvin told Johnnie Mae that she could come and that he would leave a pass for her to get in. Johnnie Mae said, Sam, this is Momma Rose grandson, Melvin. I was excited but, me, being 15 years old, I wasn't about to act like a girl and get giddy. I wanted to go to see the Temptations but I didn't have the money and I dare not ask.

We grew up in a loving diverse neighborhood. In the next block West of the Lovett's, lived the popular gospel singing family The Davis Family, I can call out some names of our neighbors who were like family members. Some were Thelma and Velma, Vera, Horace and Joseph Jordan. The Hughes, Lottie Ann, Preston and Inez and other sisters. William (Billy) Chancy. Johnnie Mae and Bop, Joann and Mary Carter, Rochell and Marquitta Rackley, Bubba Lamart, Runell, Brenda, Larry (old folks) Jean, Charles, Mamie, Patricia, Daviette, Dan, Loretta, Linda, Samuel Bernard, Joseph, Nita, Rosetta, Hazel, Bubba Jim, Joseph Michael, Toot, Ella Ree, Chopper, Willie James, Ms. Odell (Odell's Cafe), Michael Hoyt, Ronnie Hoyt, Beverly, Demetrius, Mickey Pat, William Steen, Alvin and LaGrand, Emanuel, Tommy, Naomi, Samuel Michael, Elizabeth, Tyrone Thomas, Patricia, Geno and Otis Miller, Preston Miller, Mary and Martha Ann, Carolyn, Arthur, Michael, Lawrence King, Estelle King, Linda, Patricia, Willie Longmire, Boo Boo Grady, Claudia, Pee Wee, Billie.

From some of the names listed, our neighborhood was a vast village and everyone's mother, father and grandparents were everyone's mother, father and grandparents. Our neighborhood produced a lot of prominent families in Mobile, such as the Lovetts of Lovett's Funeral Home, the James' of Butler's Grocery Store, the Juzangs of Juzang's Store, Ms. Willie Mae Ford of Willie Mae's Cafe, to name a few.

Also, in our neighborhood was where most of the black owned funeral homes were. There was and still is Lovett's Funeral Home, Christian Benevolent, Azalea Funeral Home, Smith & Gaston (Hodge's), Popes Funeral Home, Johnson & Allen, some of which still stands in the neighborhood that will be revitalized.

Another unique thing about our neighborhood is that we were only about five blocks away from downtown Mobile where we could run to the parades during Mardi Gras in five minutes. Alvin's relatives Sonny and Victor Lovett, have been an integral part of black Mardi Gras in Mobile where Victor served as King of M.A.M.G.A. and Sonny Lovett was a long-time member of M.A.M.G.A.

I also remember seeing Alvin Lovett on television with his own Sunday Morning 'Visions' television show, and just like now he was and still is an advocate for people in Mobile. Seeing a young black man with his own television show in Mobile Alabama was truly inspiring. As we grew into adulthood, started families and jobs, love from our neighborhood spread to all directions, from the West Coast, North, East and to surrounding cities and States across America. Even today, some 70 years, we still look at each other as family, and are truly family in Christ.

I could go on and on about our neighborhood, but I keep getting interrupted by my closest associates, doctors, pharmacies, honey do's, granddaddy do's, friend do's and lots of other things.

Alvin, I hope this will jog your memory about our wonderful neighborhood that we grew up in. I still ride through there and think God for allowing me to remember and revisit it from time to time.

Samuel McCord

"I've had the pleasure of knowing Mr. Alvin Lovett Alabama since 2016, and I've been consistently impressed by his remarkable character. Our first meeting took place at the KIA dealership in Carson, California, where I had arrived to collect a check for an advertisement in the National Congress of Black Women program booklet. The funds were being raised for scholarships, and Mr. Alabama support was invaluable.

Over the years, I returned to the dealership annually until Mr. Alabama relocated to Mobile, Alabama. During this time, I discovered that he was generously giving away a free car every year, a testament to his kindness and dedication to giving back to the community. I'm honored to have had the opportunity to witness Mr. Alabama compassion and generosity firsthand, and I'm grateful for the chance to share my experience with others."

"I've had the privilege of hosting Mr. Alvin Lovett Alabama on my radio show, 'Injustice', on @UNGRADIOSTATION, where his insights and dedication to community service left a lasting impression. In the Los Angeles, CA community, Mr. Alabama has been an invaluable partner, collaborating on various campaigns and attending numerous events to raise funds for those in need.

Now, back in his hometown of Mobile, Alabama, Mr. Alabama continues to make a profound impact. His tireless efforts to improve the lives of others are a testament to his unwavering commitment to community service. Please join me in congratulating Mr. Alabama on his remarkable achievements and selfless contributions to society."
Johnnie Mae Greene, AKA Mae Greene

Alabama Lovett is a life force to be reckoned with! He is the PERFECT example of someone always reaching for all that life has to offer as he offers himself freely to be directed by the Will of God!! He is part of our cause for mental wellness through our nonprofit.. Heres2lifeglobal.org. I came to know Alabama & his wife while attending Second Baptist Church in Los Angeles. The pastor at the time (Dr. William Epps) visualized the impact of having a monthly community event, Jazzy Fryday (an evening of live jazz & fish dinners) in Griffith Hall at Second Baptist Church. Alabama saw the vision & did all he could to support this warm community gathering! It was a smashing success & now is a part of our fundraising activities for Heres2lifeglobal.org. Several of the artists who performed there are now global ambassadors for this organization! Alvin Lovett SAW the vision & we are eternally grateful!! 988 Crisis hotline is one of the first Initiatives of H2LGLOBAL. This hotline is now offered throughout the United States. Because of supporters like Alvin Lovett. We now reach out to other countries to Campaign on making 988 a GLOBAL hotline for those in mental crisis. We've just returned from India to make new friends for the cause of mental wellness. We connected with another homeboy of Alabama's, Clarence Lott who was instrumental in introducing us to our friends in India. Hmmm...Maybe it's in the Alabama water!...but the book Alabama has written: Alabama Buttermilk..just in the title alone suggests that when we draw close to our roots & acknowledge our Maker we can help others to overcome obstacles; find strength & gratitude to living Life to its fullest & guide others to reach for the same!!

Alvin Lovett: Here's to LIFE! Here's to LOVE! Here's to YOU!!

Martha Lacroix

I'm Yolanda L Victor the daughter of the late Bishop W. W. Victor, Overseer of True Vine Miracle Temple, First Congregational of Lawndale Ministries. My Dad met Alabama round or about 2007, at a time when Alabama was selling cars for Car Pros Chrysler Jeep dealership out of Carson, Ca. Their partnership took off from the day they met.

Alabama provided resources such as fundraisers to help the ministry and families that struggled to become first-time buyers. My sons & nephews purchased their first cars from the No. 1 salesman in the city! Everyone knows Alabama here in our community. He has left a mark in the hearts of many with his expertise and plethora of knowledge. We thank you from the Victor Family, for the exchange between our father, Bishop Victor, his spiritual guidance and you, Alabama, for the knowledge and always serving the people. We Love You!
Yolanda L Victor

Al could be with us all day, and still party with us at night, but he always studied. How he got all that done is beyond me. He still always had time to give a shoulder to cry on. Many times, I went and spent the night at Al's home, because I had broken up with my boyfriend or whatever. He would offer his couch and he never bothered me, because he was very respectful to women.

That's another thing to admire about him. He never raised his voice. You never heard about him being mean or cruel. Not to women, and not to anyone. He was always a gentle spirit with a kind word. He cared about you, and he cared about your parents. Al knew everybody's mother and father. How did he do that?

I don't know when he slept because he was always studying, taking care of the community, being an activist on campus, and being an activist in the city. Really, when did he sleep? I don't know how he did it all, but he has always been an inspiration to me. Al's a real motivator. You cannot be around Al and not do things.

His inspiration carried me throughout my life. Al and my husband have the same kindred spirit, the gift of humanitarianism. It's a calling, like a ministry. Al Lovett will go down in history as a giver. Everyone in Mobile knows that, and probably in California now, and soon to be worldwide."
Janice White Burton

As the niece and favorite of Alvin Alabama Lovett, I have had the unique privilege of being part of a remarkable journey with a truly extraordinary man. I am the daughter of his brother, Britt Lovett, and while our family's story is peculiar, it has been nothing short of a blessing to be included in Uncle Al's life.

Growing up, I wasn't always around, but I firmly believe that everything happens for a reason. In recent years, especially since his retirement and return home, Uncle Al and I have become incredibly close. I make it a point to reclaim my time with him and Auntie Joyce, cherishing every moment we spend together. Over the years, Uncle Al has become more like a father to me, guiding me in both personal and professional matters.

His influence has been profound; he has groomed me to be a successful businesswoman. Uncle Al is one of the greatest men I know, possessing the drive of an ox and the mind of a genius. His wisdom flows effortlessly, and I love listening to and absorbing every word. As a young entrepreneur myself, I have gleaned invaluable advice from him, learning how to thrive and grow in my endeavors. He always tells me, "If you're connected to me, you will win," and I have taken this to heart, applying it to my business with great success.

I am a professional cosmetologist with nineteen years in the industry, specializing in hair. This experience inspired me to create a beauty product line, H.D. Essentials available at www.hautehandzsalon.co. Uncle Al has been a steadfast resource and support for my brand from day one, and I am deeply appreciative of his guidance. It is an honor to be part of his life, and I am committed to continuing the legacy of greatness that is so ingrained in our culture.

Thank you, Uncle Al, for being one of the greatest men I know.
With love, your favorite niece,
Dorcas Allen.

Alvin and I met in February 1994. My good friend Laverne Jarmon often hosted parties at her house, which was just two doors down from Alvin's aunt's place. Laverne had met Alvin before and thought he would be a good match for me, so she invited both of us to a card party. That night, Alvin and I teamed up and managed to beat everyone in the house at cards. He was tall, dark, and handsome—just my type. We exchanged numbers and started talking from there.

I soon invited him to my church, and we enjoyed each other's company immensely. Alvin loved my cooking and appreciated going to church with me. We hit it off so well from that point on. When my son went off to the military, Alvin and I decided to live together. He wanted to marry me at that point, but I was still legally married to my first husband. We lived together for ten years before we finally got married.

In 2004, Alvin's older brother, Britt Lovett, became ill due to Agent Orange exposure from his service in Vietnam, and tragically, he passed away. Alvin had to travel back to Compton from Alabama in September 2004. Instead of flying directly from Alabama to Compton, I suggested he fly into Las Vegas so we could get married there. After all of this, we ended up marrying on October 14, 2004.

Alvin has always been open about his life, sharing both the exciting and challenging moments. When he moved to California, he was trying to get his life together. After hearing his stories, I suggested he write a book about it, as he was such a go-getter, willing to do whatever it took to secure a job. He initially worked in a field where he cared for people, particularly one patient he helped for a long time. However, the mental health field proved too taxing for him, so he transitioned into car sales, which changed his life for the better.

“I love to travel and Al and I do a lot of traveling. As the #1 salesperson, he wins a lot of trips. I’ve gone places sooner than I thought we would. We may have gotten there eventually, but thanks to him working at Car Pros Kia, we can travel now. I’m retired from the LAPD after 32 years. I’m enjoying life being a housewife and taking care of him. A trip to Africa is on the bucket list. That’s something I would love to do, along with a trip to Jamaica. What I liked about Al, and what made me fall in love with him was that he was attentive and made sure that I was all right. I didn't have to argue and fight with him, and I still don’t, after all these years. We really get along. He’s a good provider for me, and for my family as well. He sees to it that things get done, and he's a very spiritual person. That helps, because we both love the Lord."

We've been together for 32 years now, and we've had a truly wonderful life. I worked for the LAPD for 30 years and am now retired. As a partner, Alvin is a remarkable man and a wonderful husband. I love him dearly and am so proud of him for taking the step to share his story. I'm thrilled to be a part of it and to be on this journey with him.

I love you, 'Alvin Alabama' Lovett. ***Your Wife,***
Joyce Lovett

CENTRAL HIGH SCHOOL REUNION
MOBILE, ALABAMA

ROLL CALL

Honoring 'Wildcats' Present at the October 2023 Central Reunion Festivities

CLASS OF 1947: *Marie Packer*

CLASS OF 1948: *Gladys Walker*

CLASS OF 1953: *Bessie Brown Alexander*

CLASS OF 1955: *Carceal Brown; Charles Stevens*

CLASS OF 1957: *Mary Q. Taylor Stevenson*

CLASS OF 1959: *Thomas McDowell; Celestine Simmons; Tate; Audrey Wolfe*

CLASS OF 1960: *Gloria Antone; Grace Wells Baker; Rosie Smith Brown; LaTonya Campbell; Idell*

Crawford; Joyce Archibald McDowell; Camilla Williams; Susie Williams

CLASS OF 1961: *Thomas Clemons; Rosie English Dees; Eddie Howard; Mary F. Mills; Joe Smiley*

CLASS OF 1962: *Laurie Battiste; Willie Alvin "Tit" Bryant; Hazel Campbell; Theresa Carraway; Samuel A. East;*

Nathaniel English Patricia Hendrix; Saundra Hubbard; Camilla Jackson; Greta Ponquinette; Edward Robison; M. Bernadette Jones Siggers; Joseph Slay, Jr.; Leonteen Stevens; Katherine Taylor; Clara Walker; Mary English Watson; Mack Williams; Lovel Andrews Wright

CLASS OF 1963: *Martha Armstrong; Rosa Brown; James Carter; Vernon Denson; Estell Irby; Gwendolyn Y. Jackson; Charles Johnson; Alfred Ladson, Jr.; Jerry Lett; James Miller; Kenneth Powell; Allen Robison; Emogene Robison; James R. Russell; Carl Wallace; Patricia Robinson Washington*

CLASS OF 1964: *Charles Bagsby; Robert Battles; Willie Mae Crosby; Katrina LeCounte Everett; James Finley; Carolyn Glover; Martha Smith Grace; Wayman R. F. Grant, Jr; Patricia A. Lett; Sylvester Lett; Rebecca Marks; Jerome "Jake" McNeil; Johnnie Rover; Dolores Sanders; Norman Sank; Elizabeth Wright; Mary Wright*

CLASS OF 1965: *Virginia Abrams; Cynthia Alexander; Charles Barron; Carolyn Beaton; Samuel L. Bettis; Daisy Smith Brown; Hattie Glover Brown; Lola Mae Brown; Henry "Bulldog" Hollie; Albert Campbell; Harold Carter, Jr.; Angie Crocheron; Tyrone T. Crandall; George Dixie; Carolyn Dortch; Terence Ellis; Barbara Gibson; Sylvia Horn; Elnora Davis Hudson; Marshall Hunt; Linda Huntington; Clinton L. Johnson; Glenna Merrell; Edward Moffatt; Rebecca Hardy Morris; Sandie*

Davis-Ogles; Delores Overton; Jackie Pair; Estella Royster; Deloris Russell; Anna Scott; Arthur Spears, Jr.; Lillian Tate; Samuel Williams, Jr.; Frank Walker; Kenneth Washington; Delores Wiley; Janice Stanley Wilkes; Nathaniel Williams

CLASS OF 1966: *Gregory Alexander, Jr.; Gloria Buskey; Equilla Roberson Campbell; Betty Clausell Chaney; Louis Colston, III; Patricia Crawford; Alvin "Ham" Cunningham; Roderick "Ricky" Davis; Sandy Ezekial; Earl "Gun" Harris; Ralph H. "Beau" Holmes; Saundra Hubbard; Fred "Perry" Jones; Lorraine Jones; Nettie Lang; Jereldean Lee; Cordelia "Deann" Harris Lett; Patricia A. Lewis; Essie Owes; Carrie Perkins; John Robinson; Joy Robinson; Alice English Rover; Diana Shackelford; Evelyn Skinner; Kermit Watson; Fannie Williams; Henry Wright*

CLASS OF 1967: *Carolyn Andrews; Janice Owes Boykin; Constance Brinkley; Rosie Chandler; Olga Daffin; Cleveland Davis; Wiley Day; Paul Dinkins; Francine Dixon; Mose Donald; Shirley Ginwright; Bessie Hayes; Marie Annette-Henry ;Gretchen Hudson; Sam Jones; Amanda King; Estelle King; Arneita Koger; Robert Tate Lee; Janie Ligon; Mattie May; Mildren May; Meredith McCants; Marvin C. McDowell; Mabel Moore; Leo Mose; Ruby L. Mose; Margaret Owens; Johnny E. Phillips, Sr.; Gilbert Preyer; Harold Ray; Jake Reed; Annette Richardson; Lonnie Robinson, Jr.; Lois B. Ruffin; Peter J. Spears, Sr.; Lee Tessie; Sarah Walker; Shirley Walker; Charlie Westry; Deloris Ward; Willie Williams; LeBaron Woodyard*

CLASS OF 1968: *Faye Alexander Cheryl Andry; Robert Anthony; Joyce Archible; Beatrice Banks; Linda Bennett; Theresa Blackston; Arnold Bush; Constance Brinkley; Cynthia Brinkley: Marcelene "Tonni" Byrd; Hubert Campbell; Deborah Carter; Gloria J. Cox; Reginald Crosby; Charlie Davis; William*

Day; Nathaniel Dubose, Jr.; Patricia English; Barbara Gibson; Grayson; Janice Haughton; Shirlene Hawthorne; Marie Annette Jackson-Henry; Vonnie McMillan Jemison; Christine Johnson; Clarence Johnson, Jr.; Patricia King; Regina May; Jacquelynne Moffett; Ray Moore; Janice Parrish; Belinda Curtis-Perryman; Deborah Peters; Sam Pugh; Annette Reeves; Patricia Richardson; Bernadette "Berny" M. Robinson; Gwendolyn Russell; Edna Jones Sanders; Charletta Taylor Sheehy; Lynda Wolfe-Smith; Synetta Stallworth; Delores Ward; Eddie L. Washington; Charles E. Williams, Sr.; Robert Williams; Shirley Marsh Williams; Joan E. Wilson; Willie Wilson; Sharon Yates

CLASS OF 1969: *Brenda Alexander; Frances Lewis Alexander; Sheryl Antone; Herman Curtis, Jr.; Gail Wright Files; Gloria Glover; Leonard Glover, Jr.; Hazel James; Israel Johnson; Betty Jones; Winston Lewis; Sylvia McCall; Vincent Nathan; Eugene "Dinky" Roberts; Gloria English-Rover; Willie M. Smith; Dorothy Ann Westbrook; Dora Williams Wilder; Nathaniel Wilder; Frances Williams; Donnie Yates*

CLASS OF 1970: *Adell Armstrong Brown; Phyllis D. Brown; Hazel Curtis; Blondine Dinkins; Joseph Dortch; Edith Wilson Graves; Melinda Howard; James Hunter; Van Doris Jones; Deborah Kennedy; Darlene Laffitte; Deborah Lucas; Rose M. King; Lorraine Kirksey; Ray Morris; Della Simmons Morris; Fannie Morrisette; Norman Nettles, Jr.; Louis Orangs, Jr.; Calandra Kirksey-Peterson; Albert B. Rodgers; James Sanders; Britt Stallworth; Gary Turner; Jerome White; Paul A. Wiggins; Diane Williams; Marilyn Wilson*

EPILOGUE

REV. BRITT MOSE LOVETT - MY MORAL COMPASS IN THIS LIFE

Rev. Britt Mose Lovett, born August 31, 1874, to parents Mr. and Mrs. Mose Lovett. Accepted Christ and joined A.M.E.Z. Church, Central Mill, AL, at an early age. In 1892, united with Bethel Spring Baptist Church and was baptized by Rev. Thad Taylor. In 1895, he united in Holy Matrimony to Miss. Jettie Hayes and to this union five children were born. Called to ministry in 1898, pastoring that same year, adding over 25,000 persons to the church through his administration. During his 60 years pastoring, he pastored for: Mt. Sinai, Alberta, AL; New Hope Baptist Church, Camden, AL; Old Zion, Coy, AL; Mt. Pleasant, Yellow Bluff, AL; Antioch, Dallas County; New Queen, Lamison, AL; Little Rock, Gosport, AL; Little St. Louis, Axis, AL; Sunflower Baptist, Sunflower, AL; Hopewell, Central Baptist and Shiloh Baptist, Mobile, Al; Mt. Pleasant Baptist for 35 years, Mobile, AL; True Vine Baptist for 44 years, Mobile, AL. The latter two churches were pastored until his death on June 27, 1963, leaving a devoted wife, four children and a host of relatives and friends. He, also, served as Treasurer of the Mobile Sunlight Association for a number of years. Rev. B.M. Lovett was funeralized at True Vine Baptist Church, corner of Peach and Pecan Streets, Mobile,AL. Professional services were provided by Lovett's Funeral Home, Mobile, AL. under the direction of Mr. C. T. McKinnis and Mr. W. J. Bell and followed by Interment in Oaklawn Cemetery, Mobile,AL.

So live, that when thy summons comes to
join The innumerable caravan, which moves

To that mysterious realm, where each shall take His chamber in the silent halls of death, Thou go not, like the quarry-slave at night,

Scourged to his dungeon, but, sustained, and soothed By an unfaltering trust, approach thy grave, Like one who wraps the drapery of his couch About him, and lies down in pleasant dreams. Bryant *

*Above Excerpt taken from 'Obsequies of The Late Rev. B. M. Lovett, Thursday, June 27, 1963, 1:00pm, True Vine Baptist Church, Corner of Peach and Pecan Streets., Mobile, Ala.'.

Sonny Lovett and
Victor Lovett

Vanessa Williams and
Alvin Lovett

Alvin Lovett, Dolores Williams
and Louis Williams

Alvin Lovett, LaWanda Barnes
and Carl Boyd

Tamika Williams and
Alvin Lovett-Williams

Phillip Wilson, Courtney Mierez
and Alvin Lovett

BAI HIV-AIDS Testing Van

Alvin Lovett, Maxine Waters,
Evan Wish and Phillip Wilson

Alvin Lovett and
Obba Babatunde

Alvin Lovett and Phillip Wilson

Jesse Jackson and
Alvin Lovett
MLK National Holiday

John and Janice Burton

Gina Belafonte and Alabama
HEROES in the Struggle
Fighting AIDS

Terrence Howard and Alabama
HEROES in the Struggle
Fighting AIDS

Danny Glover and Alabama
HEROES in the Struggle
Fighting AIDS

Alfre Woodard and Alabama
HEROES in the Struggle
Fighting AIDS

Taraji P. Henson
HEROES in the Struggle
Fighting AIDS

Alvin Lovett, Joey Davis and Pepe

LaVon and Gloria Banks

Women Cancer Donation

The Lovett Family Alvin and Joyce

Blake Griffin and Alvin Lovett

Danyell and Reggie Eberhardt

Stars Support The Black Aids Institute

Alvin Lovett

Chadwick Boseman and
Alvin Lovett

Phillip Wilson, Lee Daniels
and Jessie Smollett

Joyce Lovett, Reggie Eberhardt
Danyell Eberhardt and Alvin
Lovett

Brandie Singleton

A.C. Green and
Alvin Lovett

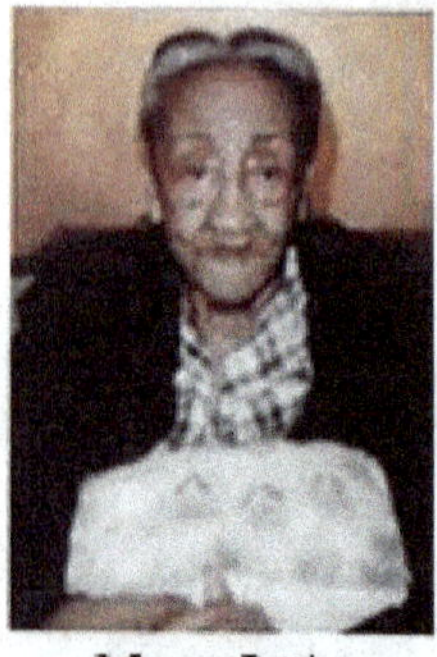

Mama Jettie
Lovett

Grandpa Mose

Great Grandfdather
Rev. B.M. Lovett

Lillian and W.J.
Lovett

Mose and Alfey
Lovett

Britt M. Lovett Sr
(Pop)

William La Grand Lovett

Britt Mose Lovett Jr.

Enobahkare Malik Peterson

Jumaane Khaild Perterson
and children

Kemba Lalita Peterson

Alvin Lovett and
Rainelle Saunders

Niki Giovanni

Joyce Lovett

Alvin Lovett

George Smith and Alvin Lovett

Delilah Kohan and Alvin Lovett

Alvin and Joyce Lovett,
Mo'Nique and Sidney Hicks

Joyce Lovett and Sheryl Lee Ralph

Baneshia M. Eberhardt

Arron Mitchell

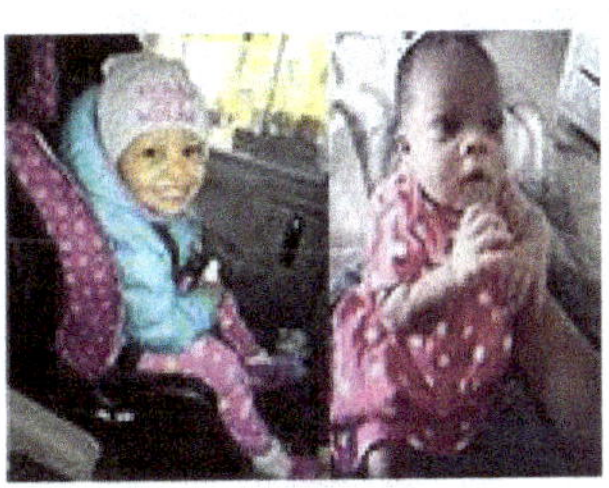

NaVaeh NaShay Eberhardt
and Kali Elaine Johnson

Rainelle Saunders

Joyce Lovett and
Gloria Wiggins Banks

Gladys Reese and Alvin Lovett
WALA TV10 NBC " Visions"

Douglas And Dorcas Allen

Britt DeVaughn Lovett

Willie Mae Donaldson and Cathy Lucas

Annie, Jettie, Kate and Willie Mae

Evans Family
Donya, David, Braxton and Brianna

Arron Mitchell Jr., Alvin Lovett and Darryl Mitchell

Angie Mitchell and Alvin Lovett

Central High School Class of 1970

John and Janice Burton,
Shawn and Leroy Bosby

Hudson, Fatima, Victor,
Alvin and Mohammad

Alvin and Joyce Lovett with
James Worthy

Frederick Allen
Graphic Designer

(His Sheltering Arms) Alabama Donates Van for Homeless Women and Children in Watts

Lillian Jeffries, executive director of His Sheltering Arms, is all smiles after receiving the keys to a new van donated to her non-profit organization by Alvin Lovett. The van was donated to Lovett by Col. J. R. Jordan, one of his clients at the Carson-based Car Pros Chrysler Jeep dealership.

Local Businessman Donates to Community Programs

Alvin "Alabama" Lovett, third from left, presented the City Council with a check for $1,000 to be put toward youth programs. Lovett, who works for a car dealership in Carson, offers Compton residents and employees a discount when they purchase a car from him. He gives the city $100 per vehicle he sells this way. (See ad on page 8)

THE LOVETT'S BOYS

Britt Mose Lovett Jr

William La Grand Lovett

Alvin Louis Lovett

Mose Lovett
Grandpa

Britt M. Lovett Sr
Father

Great Grandfdather
Rev. B.M. Lovett

Alvin Louis Lovett

Alvin Williams Lovett
Son

Taymar Johnson
Grandson

ALVIN LOVETT SIX GENERATION

ALVIN'S FAMILY

Brandie Singleton
Daughter

Donya Lambert
Niece

Dorcas Allen
Niece

Dear Readers,

From the bottom of our hearts, we want to extend our deepest gratitude to each and every one of you who took the time to read Alabama Buttermilk. Your support means more to us than words can fully express.

This book is more than just a collection of stories—it's a reflection of the legacy, love, and lessons that shaped our lives. Sharing these memories with you has been an honor, and knowing they've resonated with so many is both humbling and inspiring.

To those who have reached out with kind words, shared the book with others, or simply carried its message in your hearts—we thank you. Your encouragement reminds us why we chose to tell this story.

On behalf of myself and my wife Joyce, thank you for being a part of this journey. We pray that Alabama Buttermilk not only gave you a glimpse into our history but also reminded you of the beauty found in your own.

God bless you all,

Alvin 'Alabama' & Joyce Lovett

THE QUEEN

THE NEW JOYCE ELAINE EBERHARDT LOVETT

Works Cited

Piper, Edwin Ford. “March Wind.” *Poetry*, vol. 17, no. 6, Mar. 1921, pp. 318–320 (p87).

Guest, E. A. (n.d.). *It couldn’t be done. Poetry Foundation.* Retrieved May 1, 2025, from https://www.poetryfoundation.org/poems/44314/it-couldnt-be-done (p90)

Walk by Faith Worldwide, LLC | www.wbyf.site

Author - Alvin ‘Alabama’ Lovett

Find additional resources, books and videos on our website, alabamabuttermilk.com

Alabama Buttermilk by Alvin L. Lovett

alvin.alabama.lovett

AlvinLovet69769

Alvinalabamalovett

Alvin Lovett

www.ingramcontent.com/pod-product-compliance
Lightning Source LLC
LaVergne TN
LVHW020617110826
845149LV00002B/502

* 9 7 8 1 9 7 2 7 6 0 0 4 8 *